Praise for *ZIG ZAG*

"Finally! A creativity advice book that is grounded in scientific research."

—Mihaly Csikszentmihalyi, author, *Flow: The Psychology of Optimal Experience*

"Zig Zag is the most fun and most useful creativity book I have ever read. Keith Sawyer's gem sweeps you up with a host of great stories, quizzes, exercises, and teaches you one way after the other to be more creative."

—Robert I. Sutton, professor of Management Science, Stanford University; author, *Good Boss, Bad Boss and The No Asshole Rule*

"In geometry the shortest distance between two points is a straight line. But in creative pursuits, *Zig Zag* shows us, it's anything but. Keith Sawyer is the most creative person writing about creativity I know."

—Robert Mankoff, cartoon editor, *The New Yorker*; author, *The Naked Cartoonist: A New Way to Enhance Your Creativity*

"Creativity is essential in our journey to the future, and this gem of a book helps each of us on the way."

—Tim Brown, CEO and president, IDEO; author, *Change by Design: How Design Thinking Transforms Organizations and Inspires Innovation*

"Keith Sawyer is the best combination of a brilliant creativity researcher and storyteller around."

—Peter Sims, author, *Little Bets: How Breakthrough Ideas Emerge from Small Discoveries*

"*Zig Zag* reveals the true nature of the creative process: improvisational, surprising, with unexpected twists and turns. The book is filled with hands-on activities that help you manage that process and keep it moving forward to a successful creative outcome."

—Josh Linkner, author, *Disciplined Dreaming: A Proven System to Drive Breakthrough Creativity*

JB JOSSEY-BASS™

A Wiley Brand

THE SURPRISING PATH TO GREATER CREATIVITY

Keith Sawyer

WILEY

Cover design by John Hamilton
Cover image: © Alicat/iStockphoto

Published by Jossey-Bass
A Wiley Imprint
One Montgomery Street, Suite 1200, San Francisco, CA 94104-4594—www.josseybass.com

The collaborative sketching figure in Chapter 8 is adapted from figure 2 on page 170 of; Shah, J. J. et al. (2001). Collaborative sketching (C-Sketch). *Journal of Creative Behavior*, 35(3), 168–198. Copyright © Wiley; reprinted with permission.

Jossey-Bass books and products are available through most bookstores. To contact Jossey-Bass directly call our Customer Care Department within the U.S. at 800-956-7739, outside the U.S. at 317-572-3986, or fax 317-572-4002.

Wiley publishes in a variety of print and electronic formats and by print-on-demand. Some material included with standard print versions of this book may not be included in e-books or in print-on-demand. If this book refers to media such as a CD or DVD that is not included in the version you purchased, you may download this material at http://booksupport.wiley.com. For more information about Wiley products, visit www.wiley.com.

Library of Congress Cataloging-in-Publication Data
Sawyer, R. Keith (Robert Keith)
  Zig zag : the surprising path to greater creativity / by R. Keith Sawyer, Ph.D.
    pages cm
  Includes bibliographical references and index.
  ISBN 978-1-118-29770-4 (cloth), 978-1-118-53911-8 (ebk.), 978-1-118-53922-4 (ebk.), 978-1-118-53926-2 (ebk.)
  1. Creative ability. I. Title. II. Title: Zig zag.
  BF408.S288 2013
  153.3′5—dc23
                                                                    2012042028

Printed in the United States of America
FIRST EDITION

HB Printing 10 9 8 7 6 5 4 3 2 1

Contents

To my son, Graham

Zig Zag

Introduction

Choosing Creativity

> Ineffective people live day after day with unused potential. They experience synergy only in small, peripheral ways in their lives. But creative experiences can be produced regularly, consistently, almost daily in people's lives. It requires enormous personal security and openness and a spirit of adventure.
>
> **Stephen Covey**

Creativity doesn't always come naturally to us. By definition, creativity is something new and different; and although novelty is exciting, it can also be a little scary. We're taught to choose what's familiar, to do what's been done a thousand times before. Soon we're so used to staying in that well-worn rut that venturing into new terrain seems an enormous and risky departure.

But rest assured—you already have what it takes to be creative. Neuroscience and psychology have proven that all human beings, unless their brain has been seriously damaged, possess the same mental building blocks that inventive minds stack high to produce works of genius. That creative power you find so breathtaking, when you see it tapped by others, lives just as surely within you. You only have to take out those blocks and start playing with them. How, though?

In fact, the journey's pretty simple. In this book, I share with you the eight steps that are involved in being creative. Once those steps become second nature to you, creativity won't seem rare and magical and daunting. You'll stop being scared of writer's block or stupid ideas or a blank canvas or a new challenge, and your creative power will be flexible, versatile, and available in unlimited supply. All you have to do is learn how to tap it. And that's the purpose of the exercises in *Zig Zag*.

I started thinking about creativity many years ago, when I graduated from MIT with a computer science degree and found myself designing video games for Atari. Since then I've played jazz piano and studied how jazz musicians collaborate; earned a doctorate in psychology at the University of Chicago and studied how Chicago's improv companies create on the spot; researched theories of creativity in education; and studied how artists and sculptors teach creativity.

No matter what kind of creativity I studied, the process was the same. Creativity did *not* descend like a bolt of lightning that lit up the world in a single, brilliant flash. It came in tiny steps, bits of insight, and incremental changes.

Zigs and zags.

When people followed those zigs and zags, paying attention to every step along the way, ideas and revelations started flowing. Sometimes those ideas did feel like gifts, arriving unsolicited at the perfect time. But in reality, a lot of daydreaming, eclectic research, wild imagination, and hard choices had paved the way.

The creative act is nonlinear.

Josh Linkner, jazz musician and entrepreneur

It's lucky we do all have creative potential, because we need it more than we realize. You might think of creativity only in a single context, as a quality you pull out when it's time for a weekend craft project or a crazy practical joke. But you can use creativity to

- Excel at your job
- Build a successful career

- Balance professional success with a deeply fulfilling personal life
- Shape your personality, your sense of style, the way you connect with the world, and the way you are perceived
- Raise your children without dull routines, harsh words, or quick-fix bribes
- Learn effectively—not by rote memorization, but in a way that makes the knowledge part of you, so you can build on it
- Find fresh, clever, permanent solutions to nagging problems
- Make good and thoughtful decisions
- Forge interesting, sustaining friendships
- Bring about real change in your community

Think of a challenge, need, or issue that you face right now. Something that you care about and just don't know how to deal with; something that is frustrating you or feels like an impasse. Scribble this challenge on a Post-it note (now *there* was a creative product idea!) and stick it to this page. Scribble a few more, if you like; you can plaster the page with them.

Here are some examples that most of us have faced at some point in our lives:

- "My career is stuck, and I don't know how to move forward."
- "My relationship seems to be falling apart, and I don't know what's wrong."
- "I'm spending way more money than I'm making."

At your job, your problem might be more immediate and concrete:

- "I need a good idea for my next advertising campaign."
- "My company wants to market our successful product to a new type of customer, and we're not sure how we need to change the product to satisfy them."

- "I need a way to explain the latest changes in tax policy to our employees."
- "My group doesn't work together very well because no one understands what anyone else is doing."
- "At my medical practice, we're starting to get a lot of patients with the same disorder, and I can't figure out why."

In many professions, the problems can get so specific and so technical that only you know how to phrase them. As a psychology professor, I face challenges like the following:

- "How can I rewrite my scientific journal article so it's readable enough for a general audience?"
- "I need a research project compelling enough to win a National Science Foundation grant."
- "My students didn't understand a word of the reading I assigned. I need a clearer, livelier way to teach them this material."

As you read the techniques in this book, keep thinking of your Post-it challenges, and play with these techniques to find a creative solution.

The Eight Steps

I've spent more than twenty years as a research psychologist studying how creativity works. I've explored the lives of exceptional creators and learned the backstories of world-changing innovations. I've reviewed laboratory experiments that delved deep into the everyday creativity that all of us share.

To write this book, I distilled all that research into eight powerful, surprisingly simple steps. Follow them, and you zig zag your way to creativity.

This book is your personal trainer, coaching you through the eight zig zagging steps of creativity.

Much of what's been written about creativity until now has romanticized it, invoking the divine Muses or the inner child or the deep subconscious. Creativity glows like an alchemist's gold, always mysterious and just out of reach, but promising utter transformation. That's a clever trick, and people have made millions on it. They've convinced us that creativity is a rare gift conferred on a handful of special individuals, and the rest of us can only stumble along in the dark, hoping some of that glittering dust will fall on our upturned faces.

These eight steps aren't the exclusive property of exceptional individuals. I repeat: we all have these abilities. And the latest research in psychology, education, and neuroscience shows that they can, without a doubt, be practiced and strengthened.

This book is your personal trainer, coaching you through the eight zig zagging steps of creativity. Before I started to write, I spent a long, patient year reading countless books that claimed to increase your creativity. Some of them were brand-new, some were decades

Creativity is close to 80 percent learned and acquired.

Hal Gregersen, professor at INSEAD Business School

old, and some recycled the wisdom of the ancients. Most of them contained at least some good advice; but because they weren't grounded in research, that good advice was usually mixed with myths and mistakes. Still, in just about every book, I found at least one or two hands-on activities, exercises, and games that aligned perfectly with the latest research findings on human creativity. I organized the best of these classic creativity games and exercises into the eight steps. Then I added many of my own hands-on exercises, which I created just for this book and are based on new research about successful creative thinking.

Here are the eight steps, with short descriptions so you can see how they fit together:

1. *Ask.* Creativity starts with a penetrating research question, a startling vision for a new work of art, an urgent business challenge, a predicament in your personal life. Mastering the discipline of asking means you're always looking for good problems, always seeking new inspiration. You know where you're going, and yet you're receptive to questions that emerge unexpectedly.

2. *Learn.* In a creative life, you're constantly learning, practicing, mastering, becoming an expert. You seek out knowledge not only in formal classrooms but also from mentors, experts, books, magazines, film, Web sites, nature, music, art, philosophy, science . . .

3. *Look.* You are constantly, quietly aware. You don't just see what you expect to see. You see the new, the unusual, the surprising. You see what others take for granted, and what they incorrectly assume. You expose yourself to new experiences eagerly, without hesitation; you regularly seek out new stimuli, new situations, and new information.

4. *Play.* The creative life is filled with play—the kind of unstructured activity that children engage in for the sheer joy of it. You free your mind for imagination and fantasy, letting your unconscious lead you into uncharted territory. You envision how things might be; you create alternate worlds in your mind. "The debt we owe to the play of imagination," Carl Jung wrote, "is incalculable."

5. *Think.* The creative life is filled with new ideas. Your mind tirelessly generates possibilities. You don't clamp down, because you realize most of these ideas won't pan out—at least not for the current project. But successful creativity is a numbers game: when you have tons of ideas, some of them are sure to be great.

6. *Fuse.* Creative minds are always bouncing ideas together, looking for unexpected combinations. Successful creativity never comes from a single idea. It always comes from many ideas in combination, whether we recognize them or not. The creative life doesn't box its concepts into separate compartments; it fuses and re-fuses them.

 7. *Choose.* A creative life is lived in balance, held steady by the constant tension between uncritical, wide-open idea generation (brainstorming, done right) and critical examination and editing. Choosing is essential, because not all ideas and combinations are ideal for your purposes. The key is to use the right criteria to critique them, so you can cull the best and discard any that would prove inferior, awkward, or a waste of your time.

 8. *Make.* In the creative life, it's not enough to just "have" ideas. You need to make good ideas a reality. You continually externalize your thoughts—and not just the polished, finished ones. You get even your rough-draft, raw ideas out into the world in some physical form, as quickly as possible. Making—a draft, a drawing, a prototype, a plan—helps you fuse your ideas, choose among them, and build on what you like.

To solve a particular problem, the simplest approach is to work through the steps in order:

Creativity is not a mystery. There are proven techniques for enhancing creativity, and they are within anyone's reach.

1. ASK   2. LEARN   3. LOOK   4. PLAY   5. THINK   6. FUSE   7. CHOOSE   8. MAKE

Other books about creativity tend to stick to this linear process: spot the need or opportunity first, then identify the problem (ask), then gather information (look), then look for ideas (think), then select an idea (choose), and finally implement the idea (make). But as psychology and neuroscience are showing us, the creative process is far richer than that—and far less rigid. When you begin to master the eight steps, you'll start to zig and zag:

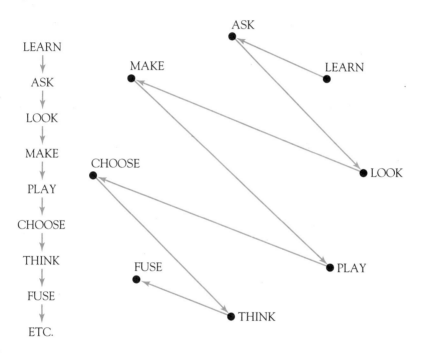

For example, although making seems to happen most naturally at the end of the eight steps, you can use its techniques to enhance the other seven steps, too. Making your ideas can help you fuse them, and choose the right ones. Making your daydreams can help you play more effectively. Making the things you see each day while looking can help you translate those sights into new ideas, or clarify your original question, or realize what you still need to discover.

Don't try to jump ahead to think and immediately have a bunch of ideas; creativity doesn't work that way. You have to follow the zigs and zags. You might not be focused on the right problem because you haven't asked the right question. You might not have the information you need because you haven't learned enough. You might not have explored the spaces and alternatives through the play that generates ideas.

Once you get comfortable with the rhythm of zigging and zagging, you'll be able to use the steps as you need them, without a rigid, linear order. In truth, any of the eight steps can play a role at any stage of creativity. After a great idea has emerged, no one can remember exactly where it started. But you can be sure that the looking continued through the final revisions, and the asking was repeated with each tiny decision about a detail in the finished work.

Exceptional creators often zig zag through all eight steps, in varying order, every day. That's part of the secret, because the steps work together to generate successful creativity. Each step feeds the other seven.

Many creativity books touch on some of these eight steps, but most of them emphasize thinking of new ideas and neglect the other seven steps. That's like waiting for a crop without sowing any seeds. If you want to do more than "be creative" for a minute or two, you need regular access to all eight steps. When you follow them, you experience a steady flow of small, good ideas. You come to expect those ideas to materialize, and they do. You can't know when they'll arrive, and you can't know what they'll look like. But you *can* trust the eight steps to bring them to you.

Zig Zag gives you, I hope, a more complete, original, and easily mastered way of seeing the world, making connections, solving problems, and overcoming obstacles. It's a handbook of proven techniques, based in solid scientific research about creativity and the brain. For my part, I've found it exhilarating to learn, with all the certainty today's neuroscience can bring, that creativity is not a mystery. There are proven techniques for enhancing creativity, and they are within anyone's reach.

Mistakes We Should All Avoid

There are two common mistakes that people make when they decide they need to be more creative. Following the zig zag way can help you avoid these errors.

Mistake #1: Thinking That You Only Need to Be Creative Occasionally

Many people think of creativity as something you need only once in a while, when your normal habits and skills fail. So you wait until you face a serious challenge, something different from anything you've ever dealt with before, and only then do you decide that creativity is the answer. You're right, of course—creativity *is* the answer. But the mistake is waiting until the last minute and then hoping to suddenly become creative, for just long enough to solve the problem at hand. As therapist and author Martha Beck once wrote, "Don't wait for catastrophe to drive you to the depth of your being. Go there now; then you'll be ready."

This process *can* help you respond to a sudden challenge, but the real benefit comes when you practice the eight steps every day. Then, instead of reacting to unexpected problems, focused on the past, you'll be finding promising opportunities that drive you forward into the future.

Mistake #2: Hoping There's One Great Idea Out There

Often we think that a creative solution to a problem will be a single thought that dawns on us in a moment of clarity. To the contrary: studies of creativity show that it rarely arrives as a single brilliant idea. Rather, creative solutions to life's problems are lit by many small creative sparks—what Virginia Woolf described as "little daily miracles, illuminations, matches struck unexpectedly in the dark." Creativity works by collecting these sparks as you zig zag forward, until suddenly they give off enough light to reveal a solution.

Wouldn't it be better to have these small sparks happening all the time, and accumulating *before* you face a serious problem? Imagine having a backlog, a notebook of good ideas that you could draw on whenever you needed it. The eight steps teach you that kind of *proactive* creativity. It's already in your power to produce this type of creativity, and it's far more effective than *reactive* creativity.

As you read this book, you'll realize why the second mistake, the "insight" myth, is so dangerous. It makes creativity sound slick and easy: the flash of insight comes, and presto change-o, your problem is solved. The danger is that when you don't have that one big flash, you conclude, "I'm not creative."

And you're wrong.

Practicing the eight steps does take some work; you have to invest a bit of effort every day to keep those small creative sparks coming. You concentrate, you commit a measure of your precious time and energy, and you persist. Luckily, the practices are more delightful than demanding, and the discipline soon comes naturally.

If creativity just meant sitting around waiting for a lightning bolt, then you wouldn't be able to learn much about it from any book. It would be inexplicable, a kind of magic outside your control. Luckily for all of us, that's *not* how creativity works. Creativity is not a trait or a property or a gift. It's a set of behaviors. "Inspiration is for amateurs," said the prolific painter Chuck Close. "The rest of us just show up and get to work."

How long will it take for the eight steps to lead you to creativity? For some people, a week or two; for others, maybe six months or a year. The time frame depends on how thoroughly you practice the steps and how readily you let old anxieties and inhibitions slip away. Once you understand the process, you can sketch more loosely, come up with better ways to communicate with your boss, or write what novelist Anne Lamott calls "shitty first drafts" without being tempted to give up—because you'll know how to choose and refine and test those early steps.

What *is* certain is that you will continue to get better at the steps. Before you know it, you will have mastered them and made them your own—custom-tailored for your own creative domain, whether it's writing fiction, working in sales, or designing computer software. As circumstances change, the rhythm of your life speeds or slows, and you experiment with new kinds of projects, you can keep tweaking. You will zig and zag your way to constant creativity, every day. The basic steps won't change, and they will never let you down.

How to Make Use of This Book

This is a practical book; it's meant to be used. The more you practice creativity, the more creative you become. So in each chapter, I take one of the eight steps, explain it, tell you why it works, and then give you *practices* that will let you master it. For each practice, there's an array of techniques, little exercises, or tricks or games that illustrate and enable you to hone that particular practice. Some you may need more than others; you'll know where to linger and when to move on. In the Conclusion, I provide additional advice about how to weave the eight steps together for maximum creativity, to finish your training as a zig zag master.

The techniques described in this handbook are not there simply to be read, tried once, and discarded with a check in the to-do box. They are there for you to use daily, in whatever way you need them. Keep the book nearby. Every day, make it a point to engage in at least one of the techniques. You'll soon find yourself doing this automatically, without even trying. But at the outset, open the book at random and choose one, or select one of the techniques matched to the step you've chosen to focus on that day.

I'd suggest you start by skimming through the book once, from start to finish. Or, you could take a quick glance at Appendix A, a concise map of all of the information in the book. That way you'll see the big picture of how the eight steps form a creative journey.

Then take the creativity assessment that follows. It will tell you which of the eight steps you're already good at, and which you'll want to shore up. That's where the techniques come in: once you've identified the steps you want to practice and polish, you can improve your creativity by using the techniques designated for each of those steps.

Personal Creativity Assessment

Give yourself one point for each "yes" answer. A higher score means you have greater potential to excel at that step. A lower score means you need a bit more effort and exercise.

Ask

_____ I am never satisfied; everything can always be made better.

_____ When someone starts telling me about a problem he or she is having, I tend to say things like, "Wait a minute; it sounds like your real problem is . . . "

_____ I get annoyed by little things that don't work like they're supposed to.

_____ I've never agreed with that old saying, "If it ain't broke, don't fix it."

_____ Sometimes I go down the wrong path, but I trust that eventually I'll catch myself and correct my course.

_____ I never have enough time to explore everything I'm interested in.

Total for Ask: _____ (6 possible points)

Learn

_____ I would call myself an expert in my area.

_____ I've learned just about everything there is to know about my creative challenge.

_____ People come to me for advice about my field.

_____ I can tell you exactly where to get the answer to your question.

_____ I stay on top of new developments in my area.

_____ I subscribe to magazines and journals that keep me up-to-date.

_____ I keep handy the most important reference books in my field.

_____ When something new and different happens in my field, it's immediately obvious to me why it's different.

Total for Learn: _____ (8 possible points)

Look

_____ I like learning new things.

_____ When I meet someone with a job I've never heard of, I ask a lot of questions about what he or she does.

_____ I dabble in things; I've tried lots of different hobbies.

_____ I get bored listening to the same style of music over and over. I seek out unusual sounds and styles.

_____ I rarely have time to watch television, but when I do, I surf channels to see what sorts of shows are on these days.

_____ I get bored going to the same places; I'd almost always rather go to a new place.

Total for Look: _____ (6 possible points)

Play

_____ Sometimes I act a bit silly, but I rarely worry about it.

_____ I often imagine what it would be like if the world were very different.

_____ I'm always trying out new things. I almost never worry about looking stupid or making mistakes.

_____ I take breaks from work, but not necessarily at exactly the same time every day. I can tell when I've worked enough and I need to clear my head, and that's when I go for coffee or a snack.

_____ I sometimes have ideas when I'm not really doing anything—in the shower, or while driving. I write them down so I can work on them later.

_____ I sometimes wonder what life is like for someone born in another country who speaks a different language and was raised in a different religion.

Total for Play: _____ (6 possible points)

Think

_____ When someone suggests a crazy idea, I'm almost always willing to go with it.

_____ I rarely have trouble coming up with ideas.

_____ Sometimes people laugh at my ideas because they seem kind of crazy.

_____ My friends and colleagues think of me as an "idea person."

_____ When someone else has an idea, my first reaction is to build on it and try to make it even better.

_____ When I can't think of a good idea, I often step back and ask, "What's blocking me?"

Total for Think: _____ (6 possible points)

Fuse

_____ I frequently notice strange connections between things—people, events, TV shows …

_____ I'm usually working on more than one project, and I switch between my projects pretty often.

_____ I like to talk to people very different from me.

_____ I'm always dabbling in new hobbies.

_____ In this past year, I attended a totally new group meeting or public event for the first time.

_____ I'm usually juggling a lot of different projects and interests.

Total for Fuse: _____ (6 possible points)

Choose

_____ I can tell pretty quickly if an idea is going to work.

_____ Even if an idea sounds bad, I can usually find a couple of good things about it.

_____ When an idea is a good one, I get a strong gut feeling, and I've learned to trust that.

_____ I've had this experience: my idea turned out to be a bad idea, but I later used that idea for a completely different problem, and it worked out in an unexpected way.

_____ Sometimes, to evaluate an idea, I'll list the pros and cons.

_____ I can tell when an idea is interesting for some reason, even if I don't know yet if it will really work.

Total for Choose: _____ (6 possible points)

Make

_____ I often doodle during phone calls or meetings.

_____ I like to fix things myself—for example, if my child's toy car breaks, or if my toaster stops working, I'll take it apart before calling a professional.

_____ I have kids' toys around that are for building things: Tinkertoys, Legos, wooden blocks . . .

_____ I always have sketches and notes posted on the wall, where I can see them and think about them some more.

_____ Sometimes, to help me think, I draw ideas or words in bubbles with arrows between them.

_____ I'm a tinkerer. I have a work area where I keep lots of tools and materials, and I'm always experimenting.

Total for Make: _____ (6 possible points)

Now that you've completed the creativity assessment, you should better understand your strengths and where you might need additional exercise. And now you're ready to begin the zig zag path, starting with the first step, ask.

THE FIRST STEP

ASK

How the Right Questions Lead to the Most Novel Answers

The most serious mistakes are not being made as a result of wrong answers. The truly dangerous thing is asking the wrong question.

Peter Drucker, management guru

In 1983 Howard Schultz was working as the head of marketing for Starbucks, a small Seattle coffee bean company. In addition to roasting their own coffee beans, the four Starbucks stores sold high-end coffeemakers, bean grinders, and other brewing supplies. In spring 1983 the company sent Schultz to Italy to attend an international housewares show, to find new, cutting-edge coffee equipment it could sell in its stores.

Walking from his Milan hotel to the convention center, Schultz passed an espresso bar. He'd never seen one before, so he went in to look around. He found a classy environment, with opera music playing in the background. But although it was classy, it nonetheless felt comfortable; the barista—the sole employee in the store, the person operating the espresso machine—knew most of the customers by name, and chatted with them as they stood at the bar drinking their espresso. Schultz was fascinated. He spent the rest of his visit checking out other espresso bars all around Milan. He discovered that some of them were upscale and some were working class, but they all seemed to be like community centers—places where neighbors would gather to relax.

In one espresso bar, he overheard a customer order a *caffé latte*; he'd never heard of it, so he decided to order one too. He watched as the barista poured a shot of espresso, steamed some milk, and topped it off with foam. After one taste, Schultz thought to himself, "This is the perfect drink. No one in America knows about this. I've got to take it back with me."

Schultz flew back from Milan to Seattle with a compelling creative challenge: "How can I recreate the Italian espresso bar in the United States?" Starbucks's three owners rejected his idea; they were happy with their successful retail business. They had no interest in turning their stores into restaurants or coffee shops. But they agreed to provide Schultz with seed money to start his own coffee shop, and they agreed to supply Schultz with their coffee beans.

Schultz left Starbucks in 1985, and in April 1986 he opened his first store, in downtown Seattle's busy business district. Going all out with his Italian vision, he called the store Il Giornale. It was truly the answer to his creative challenge: the decor was Italian, the menu had Italian words on it, and opera music was playing in the background. The baristas wore white shirts and bow ties. There were no chairs; you had to drink your coffee standing up.

Although the store was successful—three hundred customers the first day—it was obvious that the Italian model wasn't a good match with the laid-back culture of Seattle. Some people complained about the opera music, others wanted a place to sit, and virtually nobody understood the Italian on the menus. No one could even pronounce the name of the store (Eel Joe-rrnah-leh). So Schultz decided to ask a new question: "How can I create a comfortable, relaxing environment to enjoy great coffee?"

This was a much better question. After Schultz ditched the opera and Italian menus and added more chairs, Il Giornale started drawing up to one thousand customers each day. Schultz added two more stores. Just over a year after opening, the three Il Giornale stores were on track to make $1.5 million a year. Il Giornale was so successful that in August 1987 Schultz was able to buy out Starbucks, his coffee bean supplier. That gave him an opportunity to get rid of the last Italian feature of his stores: he renamed the Il Giornale stores and called them Starbucks.

The key to Schultz's success was *asking the right question*. Even outstanding creators don't know exactly what the right question is when they start out. But they're very good at paying close attention to cues that will lead them to a better question. Harvard Business School professor Clayton Christensen believes this is the secret of all successful entrepreneurs:

> Research has shown . . . that the vast majority of successful new business ventures abandoned their original business strategies when they began implementing their initial plans and learned what would and would not work in the market. . . Guessing the right strategy at the outset isn't nearly as important to success as . . . a second or third stab at getting it right.

In early 2010 the hottest thing in phone apps was location, location, location. With its built-in GPS feature, your phone could tell you all sorts of useful things, like which friends were nearby and how to find the closest public toilet (or the closest Starbucks). Foursquare had just been released for the iPhone a year earlier, and the digerati were "checking in" to let their friends know wherever they happened to be.

> You can tell whether a man is clever by his answers. You can tell whether a man is wise by his questions.
>
> *Mahfouz Naguib, Egyptian novelist and 1988 Nobel Prize winner*

A young programmer, Kevin Systrom, wanted a piece of the action. He had worked for Nextstop, Google, and an early version of Twitter, and he was ready to strike out on his own. Attracted by the success of foursquare, he started with a driving question: "How can I create a great location-sharing app?" The programming took only a few months, and the result was a simple iPhone app that let you check into a location, make plans for future location check-ins, earn points for hanging out with friends, and post pictures. Because he liked fine Kentucky bourbon whiskey, he named the app burbn.

Sad to say, it wasn't a big success. In retrospect, burbn was complicated to use, with a jumble of features that made it confusing. But around this time, a second programmer, Mike Krieger, joined Systrom. These two used a set of analytic tools to figure out what their customers were doing with burbn. Sure enough, they weren't "checking in" anywhere. But they were posting and sharing photos like crazy! Systrom and Krieger decided to ditch burbn completely and start with a new question: "How can we create a simple photo-sharing app?"

They began by studying all of the popular photography apps, and they quickly homed in on two main competitors. Hipstamatic was cool and had great filters, but it was hard to share your photos. Facebook was the king of social networking, but its iPhone app didn't have a great photo-sharing feature. Krieger and Systrom saw an opportunity to slip in between Hipstamatic and Facebook by developing an easy-to-use app that made social photo sharing simple. They chopped everything out of burbn except the photo, comment, and "like" features.

It took months of experimentation and prototyping to get everything just right. One of their early versions was called Scotch (Systrom liked scotch whisky, too) but it was slow and filled with bugs, and you couldn't use filters on your pictures. These various zigs and zags convinced them that the key to success was to make the app super easy. In their final version, you could post a photo in three clicks.

They renamed the app Instagram and launched it on October 6, 2010. On the first day, twenty-five thousand users signed up.

They hit one million users in three months. Taking an idea from Twitter, they made every photo public by default. (When the pop sensation Justin Bieber joined, thousands of girls responded to every photo he posted, causing a huge spike in Instagram activity.) By April 12, 2012, when Facebook purchased Instagram for $1 billion, it had been installed on about 10 percent of all iPhones.

When Systrom built burbn, he was driven by the question, "How can I create a great location-sharing app?" It turned out to be the wrong question. Instagram succeeded because Systrom and Krieger were willing to dive deeper into this first step, ask. They looked closely at the failure of burbn, and they used that experience to figure out their next step: they found out what their users were doing (photo sharing); they studied the existing competition (Hipstamatic and Facebook); and they came up with a new question, "How can we create a simple photo-sharing app?" The answer to that new question led to thirty million users and $1 billion. In Silicon Valley today, this kind of shift in direction is called a "pivot." I call it a zig zag.

Back in the 1970s many psychologists argued that creativity was just another name for problem solving. We now know they were wrong, because most successful creativity comes through the process that led to Instagram and Starbucks: you begin without yet knowing what the real problem is. The parameters aren't clearly specified, the goal isn't clear, and you don't even know what it would look like if you did solve the problem. It's not obvious how to apply your past experience solving other problems. And there are likely to be many different ways to approach a solution.

These grope-in-the-dark situations are the times you need creativity the most. And that's why successful creativity always starts with asking.

It's easy to see how business innovation is propelled by formulating the right question, staying open to new cues, and focusing on the right problem. But it turns out the same is true of world-class scientific creativity. "The formulation of a problem is often more essential than its solution," Albert Einstein declared. "To raise new questions, new possibilities, to regard old problems from a new angle, requires creative imagination and marks real advances in science."

Einstein loved metaphor. "For the detective the crime is given," he concluded. "The scientist must commit his own crime as well as carry out the investigation."

If the right "crime"—the right puzzle or question—is crucial for business and scientific breakthroughs, what about breakthroughs in art or poetry or music? A great painting doesn't emerge from posing a good question—does it?

The pioneering creativity researcher Mihaly Csikszentmihalyi (Chik-sent-mee-hi), who was one of my mentors at the University of Chicago, decided to answer *that* question. He and a team of fellow psychologists from the University of Chicago spent a year at the School of the Art Institute of Chicago, one of the top art schools in the United States. "How do creative works come into being?" they wanted to know. They set up an "experimental studio" in which they positioned two tables. One was empty, the other laden with a variety of objects, including a bunch of grapes, a steel gearshift, a velvet hat, a brass horn, an antique book, and a glass prism. They then recruited thirty-one student artists and instructed them to choose several items, position them any way they liked on the empty table, and draw the arrangement.

After observing the artists, Csikszentmihalyi was able to identify two distinct artistic approaches. One group took only a few minutes to select and pose the objects. They spent another couple of minutes sketching an overall composition and the rest of their time refining, shading, and adding details to the composition. Their approach was to formulate a visual problem quickly and then invest their effort in solving that problem.

The second group could not have been more different. These artists spent five or ten minutes examining the objects, turning them around to view them from all angles. After they made their choices, they often changed their mind, went back to the table, and replaced one object with another. They drew the arrangement for twenty or thirty minutes and then changed their mind again, rearranged the objects, and erased and completely redrew their sketch. After up to an hour like this, students in this group settled on an idea and finished the drawing in five or ten minutes. Unlike the first group—which spent most of the time *solving* a visual problem—this group was *searching* for a visual problem. The research team called this a "problem-finding" creative style.

Which artists' work was more creative: that of the problem solvers or that of the problem finders? Csikszentmihalyi asked a team of five Art Institute professors to rate the creativity of each drawing. With few exceptions, the problem finders' drawings were judged far more creative than the problem solvers'—even though their exploratory process left them much less time to devote to the final image, which was all the judges (who knew nothing of the process involved) were evaluating.

Exceptional creators ask questions no one has thought of before.

The most creative artists were those who focused on asking the right question.

Six years after the students graduated, Csikszentmihalyi tracked them down to find out who had the most successful careers and who were most respected by art critics. About half of the students he'd observed had stopped doing art altogether. Another quarter were recognized as somewhat successful artists. The most successful of the students, 29 percent of them, had become well known in the art world, with work in leading New York galleries and even in the permanent collections of famous museums. And these successful artists were by and large the problem finders back when they were in art school. They were the artists who focused on asking the right question.

The Practices

Creativity starts with a penetrating research question, a startling vision for a new work of art, an urgent business challenge, a predicament in your personal life. Mastering the discipline of asking means you're always looking for good problems, always seeking new inspiration. You know where you're going, and yet you're receptive to questions that emerge unexpectedly.

> Judge a man by his questions rather than his answers.
>
> *Pierre-Marc-Gaston de Lévis,*
> *duke of Lévis (1764–1830)*

The three practices in this chapter—Find the Question, Search the Space, and Transform the Problem—train you to master this critical first step. They help you ask the kinds of questions that lead to successful creativity. Exceptional creators don't just solve easy, familiar problems, such as "How can we make a smaller, cheaper cell phone?" Exceptional creators ask questions no one has thought of before. Like Csikszentmihalyi's successful artists, they are problem finders, not simply problem solvers. These practices will take you from asking yourself familiar and obvious questions like "How can I get a bigger raise?" to challenging yourself with questions like "What alternate sources of income can I identify?" or "How can I cut my monthly expenses without giving up what matters to me?" or "Do I have skills I'm not taking advantage of?"

The First Practice of Asking: Find the Question

You're set up to fail if you spend all your time chasing the answer to the wrong question. Had Kevin Systrom and Mike Krieger doggedly continued to refine burbn, their location check-in app, they would have missed the opportunity to deliver a great photo-sharing app. Had Howard Schultz stuck to selling coffee beans and coffeemakers, we wouldn't be starting our day by asking a guy with an interesting tattoo to fix us a triple, skinny, venti, Pike's Place Roast mocha latte with a shot of peppermint but no whipped cream, poured macchiato style, with espresso in the foam.

How do you find the right question? The techniques of this first practice help you generate a *lot* of good questions, some of which will lead you to surprising versions of the problem. Interestingly, research has shown that these surprising versions are the ones most likely to lead to creativity. Problem finding requires you to loosen up, like a jazz musician or an improv actor, and figure out what you're going to create. It's not an agenda-driven process; you're not handed the problem and told to follow a certain procedure to solve it. You're creating as you go.

 Try Ten Questions

Write down ten different formulations of your problem, all in one sitting. Try to make them as different as possible from each other. It's important to do this quickly, without taking a break, because working fast will force your unconscious mind to generate an odder, more intriguing mix of ideas. If you spend too much time thinking about your list, your conscious mind will start to censor the ideas, and you'll get only ideas that are "sensible"—rather than surprising and original.

I applied this method to a classic problem: "How can I build a better mousetrap?" Here are my questions:

1. How do I get the mice out of my house?
2. How do I catch mice?
3. Why are there mice in my house in the first place?
4. How did they get in?
5. What is the best way to kill a mouse?
6. How can I keep the mice from getting inside in the first place?

7. Why do mice exist in the first place, and how can we force them into extinction?

8. What does a mouse want? How can I make my backyard more attractive than the inside of my house?

9. How can we persuade all the mice to leave our neighborhood?

10. What if mice were so expensive that bounty hunters roamed the neighborhood looking for them? How can I raise the price of mice?

These versions of the problem are far from perfect—I really did make them up in two minutes—but that's okay. As you'll see, I'm on my way to some unexpected solutions.

Think of at least ten questions about cardboard boxes. I'll get you started with the first question:

1. What did people use before cardboard boxes were invented?

2. _____

3. _____

4. _____

5. _____

6. _____

7. _____

8. _____

9. _____

10. _____

Whenever you try this technique, you'll find that your questions group into clusters around common themes. Look for the two or three most promising themes. From my list, I'd pick—tempting as extinction might be—catching mice, keeping them out of the house by sealing it, and making the backyard more attractive to them.

It's likely that one of the ten new versions of your problem will turn out to be a better question than your original. For me, it's pretty obvious that the best approach is to keep the mice out of the house. So now I have a brand-new problem to tackle, a far cry from my original challenge of building a better mousetrap.

 Find the Bug

Computer programmers call annoying program errors "bugs"; when they're "debugging," they're actually finding and fixing errors. Debugging can be a boost to creativity—and a good way to come up with questions—because tiny annoyances are often symptoms of bigger problems. You can practice debugging by thinking of a product you use every day: your refrigerator, your toothbrush, your car keys, even your bathroom toilet. Now, write down every disadvantage you can think of. The product's flaws don't all have to make sense. Be unreasonable, be unfair, go on the attack. My toilet occasionally overflows; the seat is always up or down at the wrong time; it's cold in winter; the rim is awkward to clean; sitting there is boring; the flush is so loud it's embarrassing. Once you have a list, think of ways to get rid of the bugs, to make the product more efficient or more pleasant to use.

If I were to choose a mousetrap as my everyday item, I'd have no trouble coming up with bugs: the traps are hard to set; they snap on your fingers; the mice escape with the cheese or run around the house dragging the trap when it snaps on their tail. The inventors of the glue trap actually did invent a "better mousetrap" by banishing these bugs one by one. Their trap—just a plastic tray with a thin layer of powerful glue—has no painful spring mechanism and no need for cheese, and the mice can never escape once they're stuck in the powerful glue.

Still, I can't stand watching the little guys struggle, glued to that tray. So I found an ingenious *humane* mousetrap, a little tunnel, baited with generous smears of peanut butter, that tilts down and closes the minute a mouse runs inside. Once the mouse is inside, I just carry the trap to the backyard and release the mouse back into nature. Then my redefined, important problem kicks in: keeping that mouse from getting back inside!

A friend of mine tried debugging her bathroom cabinet. She was tired of having to knock down vitamin bottles and shove aside toothpaste tubes to see what was in the back of the cabinet, so she put in a lazy Susan she could spin. She was annoyed by the chore of sticking down contact paper or watching shelf paper crumple, and the woven plastic mesh she'd tried instead kept rucking up instead of laying flat. So she found a thick, soft, easy-to-clean epoxy paint that protected the shelves once and for all. Tiny changes, but she noticed them daily, and instead of that brief flash of annoyance, she enjoyed a few seconds of satisfaction that inspired her to start debugging the rest of her life.

She also told a friend about debugging little annoyances, and he went home and glared at the racks holding his collection of antique long guns. The guns' barrels slid back and forth in the top part of the rack, which risked scratching and jostling them. He debugged by inserting a flat magnet at the back of each slot, and magnets now hold the guns securely in place.

Here's a bigger debugging success story, one that not only generated a good question but also led to a prizewinning solution. Corne is a Belgian company that manufactures paper used for packaging food. In the United States, most supermarkets sell meat and cheese prepackaged, but in Europe it's still common to select your pound of bacon or wedge of Irish cheddar and then have it wrapped. Corne was starting its annual exercise to look for product improvements. Its top executives asked the creativity firm New Shoes Today to help.

The New Shoes consultants used the technique Find the Bug to generate ideas to make the wrapping paper more appealing. One person in the group began by saying, "It's boring: the sheets are too square shaped." That didn't lead anywhere; after all, wrapping paper doesn't need to be exciting. But with that idea still on the table, another person complained: "When I get home from shopping, I have all of these wrapped packages and I can't tell what's in them. I end up opening the cheese and the chicken before I finally find the salami." Bingo! Instead of "How can we make this product more appealing?" the new question was: "How can we know what's in the package without opening it?" And once they asked that question, the creative solution came pretty quickly: put a small window in the paper to reveal what's inside. This new product was released as the Duxon brand, and it was the first wrapping paper to have a window. Corne won a Packaging Oscar award for the idea. (Yes, there are Oscars for the packaging industry!)

It's doubtful that the consulting firm would have reached its creative solution without *asking the right question.*

Steve Jobs, Expert Bug Finder

Some of the world's most famous creators are particularly good at swatting away little annoying bugs that reduce the quality of our experience. The late Steve Jobs, founder and CEO of Apple, was famous for his focus on the bugs that detracted from a user's experience of a product. This sort of focus might seem too picky and narrow to result in creativity, but Jobs had one of the most creative business minds in history. It's not because he invented radically new products; all of Apple's products were new versions of products that already existed. The Macintosh computer was a variant of one already developed at Xerox; the iPod was not even the second or third MP3 player on the market. But Jobs was brilliant at finding the bugs in the user experience and removing them. The first Mac's menus, windows, and mouse were easy to use, so you didn't have to be an MIT graduate to navigate the computer; the first iMac was designed to remove all of the bugs that made it difficult to connect to the Internet; and with the iPhone, Jobs famously insisted on glass instead of plastic, so his keys wouldn't scratch the screen.

 Reinterpret

I began this chapter with two success stories, Starbucks and Instagram. What they have in common is that a product was created, and then was modified and reinterpreted as a very different product. If only Systrom could have jumped straight to Instagram without hitting the dead end of the burbn app! But that's not the way creativity usually works. Before you can arrive at the right question, you often have to go ahead and make something, then reinterpret it as something very different based on what happened when you made it. For example, let's say you're preparing a fancy dessert, a whipped cream cake coated with strawberries. You figure out a way to carefully place the strawberries on the cake, using a thin wooden skewer to get each one nestled close to the others. Later, you're putting batteries in your son's toy, and you drop one of the screws down inside the dishwasher. Remembering your strawberry skewer technique, you take out the gum you've been chewing, stick it on the end of a skewer, and reach deep into the dishwasher and retrieve the screw by sticking your gum to it. By changing the context, you've repurposed your skewer idea and created a practical new device.

Here's a technique to help you get better at reinterpreting what you've created. I've done this exercise in workshops with thousands of people, and I've learned that anyone can do it—no artistic or technical ability is required.

Start by selecting three numbers at random, between one and fifteen. Then choose a number between one and eight. Write all four numbers on a sheet of paper. Use the first three numbers to identify three shapes from the numbered display shown here:

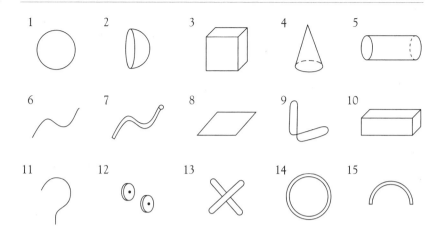

Figure reprinted by permission of L. Erlbaum Associates

Now take one minute to assemble your three shapes into an interesting, potentially useful object, and sketch it. You can combine the parts in any way, and you can vary their size. You can put some of the parts inside of others, if you like, and the parts can be made of any material. The only rule is that you can't deform any of the shapes (except for the wire and the tube, numbers six and seven, which can be bent and stretched any way you want), and you have to use all three parts in your design.

Once you've finished your sketch, take the fourth number—the one between one and eight—and pick a category from the following list:

1. Furniture
2. Personal items
3. Transportation
4. Scientific instruments
5. Appliances
6. Tools and utensils
7. Weapons
8. Toys and games

Next, take your design and rethink it, so it fits the category you chose. Don't redraw the design, just rethink your object's function. It won't be easy, but force yourself to find a use for your object within that category.

In one of my creativity seminars, one woman chose four, seven, and thirteen. She put the cone with the open end up, and she put the tube under it, extending down to the X-cross as a base. It was a flower vase, and she had even penciled in lines representing the flower stalks. She groaned when she realized she'd chosen the weapons category, but she gamely rethought her flower vase as a poison sprayer: you fill the cone with poison and swing it at your opponents, spraying poison over a large area.

The point to this silliness? Researchers at the University of Texas studied this exercise closely. They learned that when people are forced to change the context for what they've designed, they wind up being much more creative than those who knew their category ahead of time and designed an object to match. A panel of independent judges rated the creativity of each invention, and they found, consistently, that being required to reinterpret your initial sketch results in a more creative invention. Why? Because you're forced out of your first assumptions, and you have no choice but to look for surprising new connections and perspectives. Whether you're a programmer working on Instagram and seeking the creative pot of gold or a high school teacher struggling to expand your professional skills, reinterpreting what you've already done can be a powerful way to move forward.

 Rise to the Occasion

You don't have to reinvent the wheel (or coffee or photo sharing) to arrive at good questions. In fact, throughout history the same questions have kept coming up. The CIA developed a checklist of good questions that they call Phoenix. Here is my condensed (and paraphrased) version of the CIA list:

1. Why does this problem need to be solved?
2. What benefits come from solving the problem?

3. What don't you understand yet?

4. What information do you have? Is it sufficient? Is it contradictory?

5. Put a boundary around the problem—be clear about what is *not* the problem.

6. What are the various parts of the problem? Identify and describe the relationships among the parts.

7. What cannot be changed about this problem? (Don't assume something can't be changed when in fact it can.)

8. Think of another case of this same problem, but perhaps in a slightly different form, or in a different area altogether. Can you use the same solution, analogically? If not, can you use a component of the solution, or the method that led to that solution?

Here's what I came up with when, at the risk of overkill, I applied the CIA's method to my mice:

Each time you ask a question that leads to a creative solution, write it down so you can use it again later.

1. *Why does this problem need to be solved?* Because mice are unsanitary, and they're in the kitchen cabinets busting into my wife's flour and sugar and my Honey Nut Cheerios.

2. *What benefits come from solving the problem?* If I get rid of the mice, my family's food will be safe from germs and unsightly mouse droppings.

3. *What don't I understand yet?* I don't understand how these critters are getting into the house.

4. *What information do I have?* I know the mice are in the house because I find food bags torn open, and I find mouse droppings.

5. *Put a boundary around the problem.* I can't destroy the house; I can't endanger my family's safety by poisoning the food in our pantry to kill the mice.

6. *What are the various parts of the problem?* Keeping the mice out; killing the mice if they get in; protecting the food so it's harder for the mice to get to it.

7. *What things cannot be changed about this problem?* I absolutely cannot tolerate a mouse in the house (even if it's *not* eating my cereal or shredding my soap).

8. *Think of another case of this same problem.* Years ago I had ants streaming into my kitchen. I couldn't seal up all the gaps in my house because the ants were too small and there were too many tiny ways to get in. The solution was to place poison on the anthills outside the house.

The original Phoenix list features more than forty questions, including "How will you know when you have succeeded?" and "Can you use this problem to solve some other problems?"

You can personalize and extend the list by formulating your own good questions. Each time you ask a question that leads to a creative solution, write it down so you can use it again later. The first question I added was "Can I think of someone else who might have already solved a similar problem, even if the context was very different?"

The Second Practice of Asking: Search the Space

Sometimes you can't move forward because you're focused on one tiny part of the territory and the creative solution is off in a different area. Let's say you spent all of your time thinking about how to build a better mousetrap. You were exploring only one small corner in the space of potential solutions. If the most creative solution is to figure out how to keep the mice from entering your house, that's a completely different area of the solution space, and you've been ignoring it.

The techniques in this second practice are designed to help you make sure you don't leave any part of the space unexamined.

Break It Down

This ingenious three-part technique helps you exhaust all possible ways to think about a problem.

First, break your problem down into as many *properties* as you can—at least four or five. Include even the most obvious, taken-for-granted ones. Here's what I thought of for a new mousetrap: material, location, method for attracting the mouse, and method for catching the mouse. Put the properties at the top of four columns, as in the chart included here.

Second, come up with *possibilities* for each property, and list them in a column under the property. It often helps to invent improbable and implausible possibilities, as we'll see in a minute.

Third, think of all of the possible *combinations* of possibilities. The power of this technique is that it gives you an enormous number of potential solutions—in the chart, with five possibilities for each of the four properties, I have 625 possible combinations! Discard the ones that are impossible to build or aren't useful, and then seriously consider the remaining combinations.

Material	Location	Attracting	Catching
Wood	Floor	Cheese	Metal spring
Plastic	Wall	Sexy mouse	Glue
Metal	Outside house	Beer	Trap door
Paper	Ceiling	Mouse cocaine	Teleportation
Fishing Net	Inside the wall	Mouse television	Masking tape

I've circled four possibilities in my chart. What would this combination look like? A sexy female mouse sits in a plastic frame outside of the house, and when the male mouse comes up to hit on her, he gets stuck in masking tape? A crazy idea, but even crazy ideas can lead to good ones. My "sexy mouse" example might generate the better idea of attracting mice with mouse pheromones, the chemicals that animals use to signal they're interested in sex. The males race into the trap, believing there's a sexy female waiting inside. Now *that* might really work!

The properties shouldn't be surface features, like color and size, that don't really contribute to the solution. Instead, choose deep, structural properties, like method for attracting and method for catching. The key to success with this technique is identifying the right set of properties.

Draw a Fishbone

When you're stumped, it may be because you haven't identified the true *cause* of the problem. The "fishbone" technique—so-called because the finished diagram looks like the skeleton of a fish—helps you detect all the possible causes of your problem. Start by writing your problem on the right side of a piece of paper. Draw a circle around it; this will be the fish's head. Then draw a straight line from the circle to the left, and draw "bone" lines above and below this central line, at forty-five-degree angles. On each of the bones, write one possible cause of the problem. The simplest, most obvious causes should be near the head, and the more complicated ones should be near the tail.

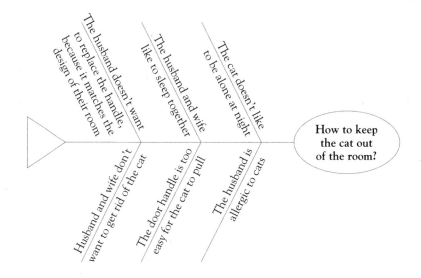

In one of my seminars, a woman talked about a problem her husband was having: her cat liked to sleep in bed with both of them, but her husband was very allergic to cats. They tried to keep the bedroom door closed, but the cat figured out how to reach up and pull down on the lever-style door handles they were using.

In the diagram included here, I've written down possible causes of this problem. Now it's easy for the couple to consider each cause in turn, and see which causes are most important, which can be easily dealt with, and which require some extra creativity.

Map Your Idea

An "idea map" is another graphic way to explore the entire space of potential solutions—and to use your mind's visual abilities to identify the real source of your problem. Here is an idea map I created for the husband's cat allergy problem:

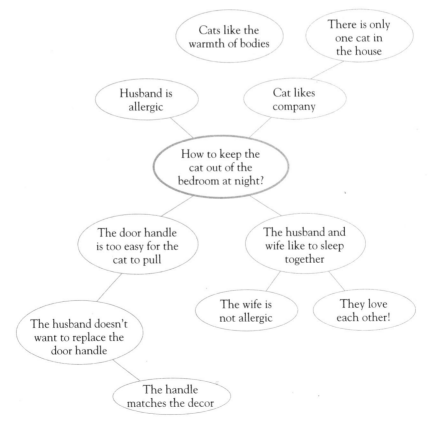

Write your creative challenge in the center of a piece of paper and draw a circle around it. It's best to have a large piece of paper, or even a flip chart or whiteboard—especially if you do this in a group. Free-associate related ideas and causes, putting each one in its own circle near the center and drawing a line linking each new idea to the original problem at the center.

You can do idea mapping on your computer, too. Try the open-source FreeMind software, available at freemind.sourceforge.net. Or use MindMeister for its Web client that supports live, collaborative idea-mapping sessions.

Other idea-mapping software includes Mindjet; MindGenius; IdeaFisher; and Visual Idea Pro. For your iPhone or iPad, try iThoughts or iMindMap.

 ## Challenge Your Assumptions

List all the assumptions you have about your problem, including the reasons you're absolutely sure it can't be changed.

A business executive who attended one of my creativity workshops started with a question that was nagging at him: "My wife's car is old and breaking down. Do I fix it or buy a new car?" Neither alternative thrilled him, so he'd been stuck for weeks. Fixing the car would cost almost as much as replacing it. But a new car's value would drop the minute his wife drove it off the lot, and deep down, she loathed cars. Traffic exasperated her; she was more prone to road rage than she'd admit; and the cost of gasoline was, pun intended, driving her crazy.

When my student challenged his assumptions, he rewrote his question again and again: Could his wife get a job within walking distance of their home? Could he? Could they share a car and take turns working from home? Could she bike or take public transportation? Could they move closer to public transportation? Luckily, because of the nature of their work, quite a few of those possibilities were feasible. They were a little more dramatic than his original, predictable question, but they were also a lot more fun to contemplate, and closer to his wife's values.

Marsha, a computer programmer, compiled her own list of assumptions—a rather bleak one, at the outset. She told me that not only was she stuck in a rut at her job but also her personal life was limited and unsatisfying. Here's what she said about . . .

- *Her career*: "Without an MBA I'll never get promoted to management."
- *Her company*: "This business is pretty stable, and our customer base is loyal."
- *Her family*: "I've always been the one who keeps everything organized."
- *Her friends and relationships*: "Pretty much, I only hang out with people I share hobbies and interests with."

I told Marsha to go through her list, and for each assumption, imagine that she's just discovered it's no longer true. I then asked her to come up with a story about how that state of affairs came to pass.

- (*"Without an MBA . . ."*) "I was promoted without an MBA. It happened when I did a stellar job on the next project, and our CEO personally sought me out."
- (*"The business is pretty stable . . ."*) "Our customers abandoned us, and our company went bankrupt. It happened when new competition emerged from Asia."
- (*"I've always kept everything organized . . ."*) "I have a lot of 'me' time, and my husband and children do a lot more of the work around the house."
- (*"I only hang out with people like me . . ."*) "I have a large group of diverse friends, and I learn new things from them every day. I met them when I joined a new church."

The Third Practice of Asking: Transform the Problem

The first two practices, Find the Question and Search the Space, help you generate long lists of problem statements. The third practice dares you to think about your challenge in a completely different way. The techniques are intended to shock you out of your assumptions.

 Reverse

In the eighteenth century physicians all over Europe stood by helplessly as four hundred thousand people perished from smallpox *every year*. The odds were pretty good that if you caught smallpox you would die, and the disease was especially brutal for children: 80 percent of children with smallpox died. One-third of all survivors went blind, and most survivors had scars from the skin infections, resulting in what was known as a disfigured or "pockmarked" face. Doctors tried curing it with herbal remedies and special cloths. One seventeenth-century doctor, Dr. Sydenham, even recommended drinking twelve bottles of beer every day! Nothing worked.

The driving question was: "How can we cure this dread disease, which is killing our citizens?" No answers came until 1796, when the British physician Edward Jenner reversed the question. Noting that the women who milked cows rarely caught smallpox, he asked, "Why do milkmaids not get smallpox?" The answer was that they were immunized by exposure to cowpox, which is relatively harmless. Jenner went on to extract some pus from a milkmaid's cowpox lesion and inject it into an eight-year-old boy, James Phipps. Two months later, he injected young James with pus he'd taken from a fresh smallpox lesion—and James did not get sick. (Phew! Give James a monument.) Jenner named his invention "vaccination" after the Latin word for cow. His enormous contribution was spurred by a simple reversal of the prevailing question—not "How can we prevent smallpox?" but "Why don't milkmaids get smallpox?"

A historic illustration of creativity via reversal comes from the automobile industry. In the early days of the business, one work team would swarm around the car, do their part of the job, then file out as the next work team came in. Factory managers kept asking, "How can I get each work team to the car faster?" Henry Ford turned the question around. "How," he asked, "can I get the car to the work team?" The answer—which gave rise to the assembly line, where the work team stayed in one place as cars were carried to them—forever changed American manufacturing.

 Go Back from the Future (BFF)

In searching for creative solutions, most people look forward from the present. Instead, why not visualize your goal, then work backward to your current situation?

One of my students was trying to lose ten pounds. She visualized herself grabbing fruit or fresh veggies whenever stress made her ravenous. That meant the fruit and veggies needed to be close at hand—as close as the cookies she currently kept in her bottom desk drawer. She dreamed up a refrigerated desk drawer, with a rubber-sealed hinged top, that would take the place of the deep file drawer in her desk.

She loved the idea—we all did—but her boss wasn't going to buy her a high-tech, customized, refrigerator-drawered desk. So she remembered a tiny refrigerator that was sitting at home in the garage, waiting for her husband to want icy sodas while he worked on his old Fiat. The Fiat was beyond repair, and the tiny refrigerator fit perfectly in her drawer, its cord running out the back and plugging into an unused outlet.

BFF has far weightier applications, of course. It's been widely used to solve technical problems of all kinds. In the 1980s scientists working on the Jupiter space probe Galileo faced a major challenge—how to create a rocket booster large enough to propel the probe to Jupiter without damaging the delicate cargo bay at launch. The creative solution came via BFF: instead of focusing on the booster design, they focused on the goal: "We've arrived at Jupiter, and with lower rocket power. How did it happen?" At first, they were stumped. They'd already failed to figure out how to make it happen. And yet, by thinking back from the future, the engineers could speculate about a way it might have happened: perhaps they could have used the gravitational force of Venus to add force to the space probe long after its launch. If they timed the launch exactly right, a relatively small booster rocket would get the probe to Venus's orbit, and the gravitational force of Venus would swing the probe around and give it the extra velocity needed to reach Jupiter.

You can use idea mapping in combination with BFF. Instead of starting with your problem at the center of the paper, start with your desired end state. What will your life be like after you've found a creative solution?

Launched in 1989, Galileo swung around Venus in 1990 and reached Jupiter on schedule in 1995, after traveling through space for five years. Galileo was an amazing feat of engineering, and BFF played a significant part in Galileo's success.

Pick the Worst Idea

This technique comes from my friends in Chicago's hottest theater scene. At the Improv Institute, the actors ask audience members to shout out "world's worst" prompts for skits. Experienced improv actors get used to hearing "world's worst boss" or "world's worst boyfriend." This technique got picked up by the TV show *Whose Line Is It Anyway?* On one show, host Drew Carey started a scene by suggesting this prompt: "World's worst thing to say on your first day in prison." The first actor's response brought down the house: "Who here loves to crochet?"

Paradoxically, bad ideas, even the "world's worst," can lead you to good ones. Start by listing the absolute worst ideas you can think of. Then try to identify potentially good features of these terrible concepts.

The marketing consultant Andy Stefanovich describes two true cases. At a toy company, he and his team came up with the idea of a "hooker doll." Truly the worst! But when the group talked about it a bit more, they realized that this doll drew on make-believe play that little girls love: dressing up, dancing, and going out on the town. When the laughter settled down, this appalling idea actually gave rise to a doll that was successful. She was given a backstory—the life of a sophisticated woman, with limos, nightclubs, and dance parties. (You can no doubt understand why the toy company wants to remain anonymous!)

At Woolmark—the wool manufacturing trade group—Stefanovich's group was charged with changing the image of wool from something your grandmother wears to a stylish, modern material. They had a small budget and a fixed schedule: the promotion would take place during New York City's high-octane fashion week. One of their "world's worst" ideas was, "Let's run a herd of sheep through Times Square and disrupt traffic." A crazy notion, but once an idea like this gets on the table, it sticks around in your subconscious. So later, when one of the team members spied a typical New York dog walker with ten dogs on ten different leashes, they knew they had found the right question: "What if we put sheep on the ends of those leashes?" And so was born the incredibly successful Sheepwalk ad campaign, in which leggy, high-cheekboned models paraded sheep up Manhattan's elegant Madison Avenue.

Writers often secretly use this technique. "Read the classics, choose fine authors, read good journalism," they tell their students. But when they need to remind

Try it yourself. Think of the world's worst way to

- Ask for a raise
- Save for retirement
- Improve your marriage

Now, do these horrible ideas give you any new insight into the problem?

themselves of the basics, nothing works better than grading beginning student essays that include tons of mistakes, or reading a lousy book and knowing just how they'd do it differently. The worst can be a creative prompt—and a confidence builder.

Stretch and Squeeze

Transform your problem by *stretching* it, to make it a broader, more universal question, or *squeezing* it, to create a narrower, more tightly focused question. These two exercises work because when you're stumped, it's often because you're pondering your problem at the wrong level of abstraction. Stretching makes it more abstract; squeezing makes it more concrete.

Stretch by using the Five Whys technique—keep asking why, up to five times, until you get to a powerful new formulation of the problem:

1. Why don't I have a girlfriend?
   (because I don't meet any women)
2. Why don't I meet any women?
   (because I have a demanding job and I have no spare time)
3. Why is my job so demanding?
   (because I enjoy it and I'm committed to the work)
4. Why am I so committed to my job?
   (because my work is making a real difference in the world)

   You know you're on the right track when the "whys" get you to a new "how" question:

5. How can I stay committed to my job and still have time to socialize more?

Now you've arrived back at a concrete question, but an entirely new one that could actually yield a creative solution. The secret is that the new question, informed by a broadened look at your life and your values, actually gets at the root cause of your dilemma. The first question turns out to be a symptom, and most likely a temporary one now that you know how to treat it.

You also need to transform your problem when it's too *big* to be solved all at once. A problem like "I'm not happy with my job" is just too sprawling and vague to solve, even for the most creative person on earth. Break it down into smaller problems by listing the reasons you're unhappy about your job:

- My commute is too long.
- The work is boring.
- My boss isn't nice to me.
- My boss wants me to be available 24/7.
- I don't make enough money.
- It's just not fulfilling.

One of these smaller problems might already suggest a solution. If not, maybe you need to take the big problem and

If you're stumped, you might be pondering your problem at the wrong level of abstraction.

squeeze it. Squeezing narrows the problem, reducing the territory you need to explore. Squeeze by asking "who," "what," "where," "when," and "how" questions. Who at your job is present when you feel unhappy? (Maybe there's a personality conflict that's coloring your entire day.) What tasks make you unhappy? (Maybe you just need to ask for more responsibilities, or different ones, or less pressure.) Where are you when you're most unhappy? (Maybe it's only at the morning meeting, because the atmosphere's so competitive and aggressive.) When does this feeling of unhappiness strike you? (Maybe it only hits on Sunday evenings and Monday mornings, and the real problem is that your weekends aren't satisfying, so you dread starting the workweek unrefreshed.) How do you react when you feel unhappy? (Are you snapping at your coworkers or retreating into a dark mood, thus feeding a vicious cycle?)

You know you're on the right track when *squeezing* gets you to a concrete statement of the problem that's so obviously accurate and specific, you're halfway to a solution already.

The risk with *squeezing*, though, is that you can end up with a question that's so narrow that it contains an invalid assumption. Maybe you squeezed your "Why don't I have a girlfriend?" question until you reached a lot of practical questions about where and how to meet more women. But these "girlfriend" questions have a built-in assumption: if you meet more women, you're more likely to find a girlfriend. Perhaps the problem isn't that you never meet women, though. Perhaps the real problem is that you act shy when you meet a woman, or you don't feel good about yourself, or you're not a lively conversationalist. Make sure to search the space before you squeeze your question.

Onward . .

Ask, the first step in your journey, just might be the most important. You'll find yourself returning to the techniques in this chapter more than those of any of the other chapters because this is where creativity begins.

Then, once you've pinpointed your creative challenge, you need to become a master, an expert in the kinds of knowledge that are related to your challenge. That sounds daunting, but I don't mean you need to master every aspect of every related field. You simply need to know how to find the information you need, hone the skills you require, and keep new inspiration streaming in. The next step is to learn.

LEARN

How to Prepare Your Mind for Constant Creativity

If you stuff yourself full of poems, essays, plays, stories, novels, films, comic strips, magazines and music, you will automatically explode every morning like Old Faithful. I have never had a dry period in my life because I feed myself well.

Ray Bradbury

In 1989 Joshua Bell received his degree in violin performance from the top-ranked Jacobs School of Music at Indiana University. Dozens of other talented students stood, robed and gowned, to receive music degrees that year, but Bell has outshone them all. He's performed at Carnegie Hall and with every major symphony orchestra. He's recorded more than thirty CDs. He's been on the *Tonight Show*, *VH1*, and *Sesame Street*. He's even appeared—as himself—in a movie starring Meryl Streep.

What makes exceptional creators different from the rest of us? Those other violinists who graduated with Bell in 1989 were incredibly talented, and many went on to have successful careers—but nothing like Bell's. Most of us live out stable and productive lives as managers, chemists, graphic designers, high school history teachers ... while a handful of creators across these and other professions transform the world with a blaze of energy. What's their secret?

The most obvious answer is that exceptional creators are born that way. That notion's almost a comfort, because if it's true, then we can only go as far as our natural ability allows. After that, we might as well relax, pop in a DVD, and grab a beer.

God-given ability was touted in the nineteenth century by Sir Francis Galton, a famous British psychologist who was a half cousin of Charles Darwin. He wrote a book in 1869 called *Hereditary Genius* and published other writings about "hereditary talent" and "hereditary success." His answer to our question would be simple: Bell just has more God-given ability.

For more than a century scientists agreed with Sir Francis: innate talent explains creativity. But surprising new research by professor Anders Ericsson—the world's leading expert on expertise—throws this classic assumption into question.

In the 1980s Ericsson set out to analyze how people reach the highest levels of human achievement. Since then he has studied thousands of world-class musicians, chess players, and athletes. What's the secret to exceptional success?

Deliberate practice.

In one of his studies, Ericsson asked all of the violinists at the Berlin music academy to keep a weekly record of how much they practiced and exactly what they did during their practice time. After their first two years in the academy, the top violinists had practiced twice as many hours as the average student!

In other studies, Ericsson discovered that the world's top violinists had invested a total of ten thousand hours honing their craft. That magic number of ten thousand hours has been observed in domains as varied as chess, medicine, programming, physics, and dance. Ericsson's research suggests rather strongly that exceptional creativity is not genetic at all. The real secret to exceptional creativity is practice.

That "ten thousand" number doesn't mean the most creative people are necessarily the oldest or the most seasoned. Tiger

Woods won the 2000 Masters Tournament when he was only twenty-one. Bell played at Carnegie Hall when he was fourteen. But Bell *started* playing violin at four, after his mother saw him stretching rubber bands across his dresser drawers and plucking out the sounds she was making on the piano. That means that by fourteen, he'd been practicing for ten years—and guess what? If you put in four hours a day, five days a week, for ten years, you've reached exactly ten thousand hours. (Studies show that you don't get any additional benefit from practicing beyond four hours a day—you lose energy and start to burn out.)

When we study the biographies of exceptional creators, we discover that Bell is not unusual.

The real secret to exceptional creativity is practice.

On average, these geniuses have each dedicated at least ten years of hard work to master their chosen profession. This "ten-year rule" was actually discovered back in 1899, when *Psychological Review* published a study showing that it takes ten years to become an expert telegrapher. But everybody was still in Sir Francis's camp, so the implications didn't become clear for another century. In 1973 cognitive psychologists Herbert Simon and William Chase estimated that international-level chess players had invested at least ten years of study. Then, Harvard psychologist Howard Gardner demonstrated that creative individuals across a wide variety of domains tended to come up with major breakthroughs after ten years of deep involvement in their chosen domain.

Bell wasn't unusual, either, in having his chubby fingers wrapped around the bow of his made-to-scale violin at age four. It turns out many exceptional creators start learning when they're quite young. Woods, for example, played his first round of golf at the age of three, and by the time he won the Masters at the age of twenty-one he had eighteen years of deliberate practice under his belt. Judit Polgár, now said to be the strongest female chess player in history, started playing as a toddler (taught by her older sister, Susan). Polgár started playing at age four, and by age fifteen she was the top-ranked woman player in the world.

When the psychologist Vera John-Steiner interviewed more than one hundred exceptional creators, she learned that they all became immersed in their area of interest at a fairly young age. Chilean poet Pablo Neruda, in his autobiography, wrote that he "gobbled up everything, indiscriminately, like an ostrich." Painter Brent Wilson, who grew up in a small, sleepy town, remembers spending hours poring over the brilliant photos in every new issue of *Life* magazine.

> Long after Woods was already a world champion, he continued to deconstruct and reconstruct his golf swing.

So is it enough to practice ten years, and do you automatically become a prodigy if you just start early? Hardly. The top performers excel because they've mastered a special kind of learning that Ericsson called *deliberate practice*. Deliberate practice isn't just playing the same song over and over, or playing scales up and down for hours each day. It requires working on tasks that are a little bit beyond what you're capable of doing, but that you can still master with concentration and feedback. You never get comfortable; you always work to get even better.

Orchestra Rehearsal

Roger Kaza, principal horn for the St. Louis Symphony orchestra, once told a reporter for *Playbill*,

> If you're doing it mindlessly, or you don't have the proper direction, you can completely waste your time. The most important thing is that you practice creatively and you're never bored. If you are just plugging away, putting in time, your body kind of knows that, and you don't get anything out of it.

Kaza uses all sorts of tricks to keep his practice deliberate and creative. He'll circle around a challenging new piece, playing it in a different key or faster than he should, "so when you do it at concert rhythm, it sounds easy." Some of his colleagues in the orchestra will videotape their hands as they play, or they'll record their practice and play it back at half time, so every mistake they've made jumps out at them.

What they won't do is slack off, so their brain chugs to a halt and their muscles lose their memory. Nor will they overpractice, so that what they're doing becomes rote, too easy, or grim and joyless. The art of being "deliberate" is practicing mindfully, just a bit ahead of your ability, and with passionate interest.

The Practices

When you master the discipline of learning, you find yourself naturally absorbing new information like a sponge. You learn everything about what has come before, what other people have tried, what has and hasn't worked. You become an expert, yet you're not limited by past ways of thinking. You're always ready to move beyond what you already know, or what the world already believes.

The four practices in this chapter—Practice Deliberately, Master Your Domain, Learn Forever, and Balance Specialty with Generality—train you to master the second step.

The First Practice of Learning: Practice Deliberately

As Anders Ericsson discovered, deliberate practice is the pathway to the highest levels of creative performance. You need deliberate practice techniques if you're working really hard at learning yet feel like you're just not getting anywhere. Plateaus are maddening—and they're not necessary. With deliberate practice, you will move forward steadily. The old Romantic notion of the fallow period, the dry spell, the creative block . . . glamorizes getting stuck. Although we've come to think of those periods as inevitable, they're not.

Exceptional creators hone their craft in a very particular way. These four techniques show you how they do it.

 Challenge Yourself

Mihaly Csikszentmihalyi's research on *flow* shows how to maximize the benefits of deliberate practice. Flow is a state of optimal experience; it's the most fulfilling way of being. People who spend more time in flow are happier with life, and they're more creative.

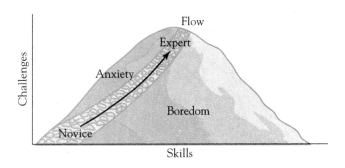

When you start to learn as a beginner, it doesn't take a very big challenge to overwhelm your skill level, because your skill level is very low. But as your skills improve, you're no longer challenged by that same task, and it becomes boring. Creative learners actively reflect on their own learning process: they notice when they're getting bored, and they seek out the next challenge. Then, gradually, they return to the flow state—but this time, further along the path to expertise.

In some situations, the challenges increase a bit before you're ready, rising above your skill level. That can make you so anxious and uncomfortable that your first, screaming instinct will be to go backward, returning to an easier challenge. But then you won't learn anything. Creative learners handle challenges differently: when they start to feel that anxiety, they work harder to improve their skills so that they can master the new challenge. Once they do, they return to the flow state, but at a higher level of expertise.

Creative learning is difficult by design: if you're doing it right, it never gets easy. Compared to top performers, people who remain amateurs spend a lot

Creative learners actively reflect on their own learning process: they notice when they're getting bored, and they seek out the next challenge.

more of their practice time on enjoyable, playful activities that do little to improve their skills. Compared to amateurs, top performers work much harder at deliberate practice.

 Focus on Specific Tasks

Break apart your problem, so you have a series of small, manageable subcomponents. Focus on each of them in turn. As you do, use a mental picture to remind yourself how that subcomponent fits into the larger context.

For example, a pianist might focus on one phrase of a melody and play it over and over to get it just right. Or the pianist might play just the left-hand part repeatedly until she's mastered it, and then play just the right-hand part, eventually putting them together. A basketball player might practice free throws for an hour, or decide to focus on layups for thirty minutes. Yet all along, these performers are holding in their mind's eye a picture of the entire composition, a strategy for the entire game.

 Reflect

Concentrate on your performance while you're learning.

- What are you doing that's working?
- What's not working?
- What can you refine or improve?

For your learning to lead to creativity, you have to be fully attentive to what you're doing, so that you notice areas of potential improvement. Deliberate practice works best with immediate feedback. Beginners don't know what to concentrate on and can't provide themselves with the appropriate feedback, so if you're just starting out, it really helps to have a coach or a teacher. As you develop increasing expertise and ability, you'll often—although not always—be able to provide yourself with the feedback you need.

Paradoxically, the world's top experts are far more critical of their own performance than of the world's amateurs. As the novelist Thomas Mann put it, "A writer is somebody for whom writing is more difficult than it is for other people." Deliberate practice leads to greater creativity, but it takes a lot of energy. You should only expect yourself to be able to do it a few hours each day; otherwise you'll just get exhausted. You need time each day to recover. Studies show that you don't get any additional benefit from practicing beyond four hours a day, and in fact some studies show that after you go more than two hours the benefits begin to decline. Coaches call this "overtraining" or "burnout."

Many creators structure their workday with a few hours of deliberate practice first thing in the morning, when their intellectual energy is at its peak. The rest of the day, they take care of work that is less demanding.

The Second Practice of Learning: Master Your Domain

Isn't it true that the experts are stuck in their ways? Don't the best ideas come from unschooled outsiders? No, in fact, they don't. Those are myths. The truth is that you have to learn an awful lot about an area before you can be creative, and school is designed to give you that knowledge.

Without some kind of structured learning, you're likely to be trapped by your assumptions, fooled by biases you didn't know you had. That's why creative mastery of a domain typically requires formal schooling. Not all classrooms are created equal, though. The four techniques of this second practice can help you get the most out of your classroom experiences.

 Get Schooled

Deliberate practice is hard to design for yourself. You really need a skilled teacher or coach who can design the learning experiences for you—particularly when you're just starting out. The genius of a talented teacher is his or her ability to sense exactly what each pupil already knows, and to creatively design an activity that's targeted just above that skill level. As pupils grow in knowledge, the creative teacher adapts right along with them, keeping the students in the flow zone.

Of course, not all teachers do this. If you find yourself in a classroom and you're bored, create additional challenges to get yourself back in the flow zone. (The same is true when you're learning on the job. If your boss is perfectly happy with what you're doing, invent your own challenges.) The real fun of learning isn't sitting there while someone dazzles and distracts and amuses you. The real fun is feeling your mind expand, seeing yourself do something with ease that just a month before would have confounded you.

Learning for Creativity

At a radical learning institution in Denmark, Aalborg University faculty have spent three decades perfecting a type of active learning called *problem-based learning*. Instead of sitting in lectures and being led through a textbook chapter by chapter, students are given a real-world problem and have to figure out how to solve it. They learn how to identify what knowledge they need, find it, and determine how to use it.

Some students don't understand why they get this strange new form of education. In one formal evaluation at the end of a semester, one student wrote, "The problem with my classes here is that I keep learning things I won't have to know until after I graduate." Of course, that's exactly what every student *should* be learning! It means you're learning deeper, which helps you creatively adapt what you've learned to a variety of real-world settings. And this is exactly what you need for successful creativity.

 Go for Deeper Understanding

Creative learning results in deeper understanding, not just memorization of surface facts. Creativity involves knowing how to think, reason, and argue—and how to explore further, ask the next question, and find the answer. When you learn this way, you're more able to use your knowledge in the real world. And because it becomes part of you, it won't fade away as soon as you pass the exam. You'll continue building on your knowledge, rather than starting over from scratch with each new problem.

If you want to learn creatively, never focus on just the facts. Seek out the underlying conceptual structure and the deeper meaning.

You might be thinking, "Knowledge is so quickly outdated, and problems change so fast, why stuff my brain with information that won't be relevant tomorrow? It's an exercise in futility." It is, if you define knowledge as a hodgepodge of facts and formulas and procedural rules. But we're not playing *Trivial Pursuit* here. Deep knowledge transcends circumstances. The difference between experts and novices isn't that experts have *more* knowledge; it's that they have *different* knowledge. Experts' brains are filled with important domain-related concepts and approaches. And because of that, when they face a creative challenge, they can quickly access the knowledge they need for a creative solution. People who are less creative are still sitting there looking puzzled and blank, because they think in terms of specific facts and methods. Their brains may be stuffed, but it's hard for them to retrieve any meaningful knowledge.

Let's take an example from middle school math, when teachers struggle to help children learn about fractions. Most children—you and I included—learned about fractions in a superficial way. I'll give you a few simple problems to show you what I mean. Start by solving this problem:

$$1/4 + 1/4 =$$

When adding fractions, you might remember that you add the two numerators and keep the denominator the same, resulting in the answer: 2/4. That makes sense; when you add two numbers, you get a bigger number—duh!

Now try this problem:

$$1/4 \times 1/4 =$$

If you remember how to multiply fractions, you'll remember to first multiply the numerators, and then multiply the denominators, getting you the answer of 1/16. Most middle school children have no problem memorizing this procedure and calculating the answer. Their minds are filled with this kind of math knowledge, but it's superficial; they rarely learn *why* the answer is 1/16. And, frankly, the answer 1/16 is pretty confusing, because it's smaller than 1/4. When you add 10 and 10, you get 20. When you multiply 10 and 10, you get 100—a much bigger number. And likewise, when you add fractions, you get a bigger number. So why does *multiplying* fractions result in a smaller number? Most children never learn the underlying meaning of what is going on when they multiply two fractions; instead, they just regurgitate the formulas on the test, and then go through life thinking that math is really confusing.

You can only understand *why* once you know the underlying meaning of what's going on when you multiply fractions: you are taking a fraction of a fraction. If you take a pizza with four slices, and then you cut each of those slices into four smaller ones, you'll end up with sixteen slices. So if you want 1/4 of one of those original four pieces of pizza, you want only 1/16 of the pie.

With deeper understanding, you know the meaning of what you're learning, and you're prepared to answer "why" questions. Exceptional creators see the world differently because they understand it more deeply. They know the universals, the principles that transcend specific situations. And that lets them spot good problems and challenging opportunities that novices look right past.

If you want to learn creatively, never focus on just the facts. Always bear in mind the underlying conceptual structure and the deeper meaning.

 ### *Apply What You Know to New Situations*

Creative learning results in what psychologists call *adaptive expertise*—an ability to apply what you know to surprising new situations. Adaptive expertise can be used to solve a wide range of problems, not just the narrow sampling you'd find in a textbook.

To build your adaptive expertise, spend time applying what you learn to wildly different situations. List as many areas as possible in which your new knowledge might apply. Notice how you can bend and stretch it to fit a new context. Maybe you're redecorating, and you've just learned a bit of color theory that explains why placing a color next to its opposite color will intensify it, making it more vibrant. You're trying to create a tranquil bedroom, so you decide *not* to pair turquoise and coral; instead, you choose soft, grayed blue-greens and white. But now you can use what you've learned to give your husband advice about bold lettering for a new sign advertising his business. You can make bouncy, attention-getting posters for your daughter's bake sale. You can choose a bouquet that will thrill your mom, whose vision is fading. You rethink your nature photographs. You plant lemon-yellow daisies next to the purple sage, instead of your usual pale pink petunias. You choose red cherry tomatoes to garnish a spinach dip.

With adaptive expertise, you don't let that bit of new knowledge suffocate in a tiny, airtight box; your knowledge runs free.

The Third Practice of Learning: Learn Forever

The creative life is fed by continuous learning. Once you've finished school, it's time to get *started.*

These five techniques show you how to create a life in which you never stop learning—and you rarely feel like it's a grind. Your mind will stay limber, stretching further every day, and the more you learn, the more connections you will see, and the easier it will be to solve problems of all kinds.

When Steven Johnson was asked to summarize the core message of his insightful book *Where Good Ideas Come From,* he said simply, "Chance favors the connected mind." And nearly any creative genius who's honest will admit that a creative block isn't some psychic fugue state; it comes because he or she hasn't learned enough, hasn't gathered enough information or inspiration, hasn't worked through the logic of what he or she is trying to do.

> The brain that doesn't feed itself eats itself.
>
> Gore Vidal

Seek Knowledge Relentlessly

Successful creators don't just like knowledge, they thirst for it. They can't stop asking questions, and they always go beyond what they've learned from teachers and books.

Whenever you're ready to learn more about your chosen domain of creativity, whether it's your everyday work or one of your many interests, keep thinking beyond:

- Watch for the sacred cows—the ideas or approaches nobody's willing to touch.

- Be ready to question the established truths you are learning.
- Take a playful approach to what you're learning. Don't take it too seriously, and always keep asking, "Why?" Three-year-olds shouldn't have all the fun; you can pester the grown-ups too. A childlike attitude helps you learn in a more creative way because it keeps the ideas alive and animated.

Don't Swallow the Beetle!

As a kid, Darwin collected beetles. One day he was tramping through the woods near his home, and he saw a beetle he didn't have in his collection. Before he could grab the beetle, it crawled under the bark of a tree. When he carefully peeled off the bark to get to the beetle, he found two more beetles that were even larger and glossier. They were all so big, he could only hold one in each little hand; so he put the third one *in his mouth* and ran home with all three beetles!

 Customize Knowledge

After Paul Maeder made himself into a successful venture capitalist, he looked around at other successful entrepreneurs and noticed a common trait: they all kept educating themselves. When they wanted to learn something, they didn't just meekly sign up for classes; they went out and got the knowledge their own way.

Take a lesson from these entrepreneurs: use every possible avenue to find knowledge that's related to your problem.

- Do an Internet search.
- Read experts' blogs and journal articles.
- Surf through Wikipedia; consult MetaFilter.
- Find an online educational video; listen to a TED talk.

- Call up a friend or colleague who might know someone who knows something about it.

Use all your senses. If you want to learn about, say, the tiny town of Mystras, Greece, of course you will read its history and travelogues. But you might also learn a little Greek; look at photographs of the Peloponnese; make one of the region's traditional dishes; listen to its music; watch videos of its Easter festival; listen to one of the region's radio stations online; shower with its olive oil soap; learn to play a Greek children's game; watch a movie set in Mystras; talk to an archaeologist who runs a dig there; e-mail Theonidas, the innkeeper at the Mystras Inn, asking him to tell you his town's stories and lore ...

Many Web sites have educational videos:

- iTunes U
- FORA.tv
- Khan Academy
- Open Yale Courses
- Expert Village channel on YouTube

Read a Book

Exceptional creators tend to be voracious readers. John Mackey, founder and longtime CEO of Whole Foods, belongs to two different monthly book clubs and reads a new book every week—while he's running a $4 billion company! If *he* can find time, you and I can too.

Exceptional creators, in all walks of life, are surrounded by books.

- Go to the library and ask a librarian for help finding relevant books, or do a keyword search using the electronic catalog.
- Search on Amazon.com or Barnes & Noble's Web site for keywords related to your problem. When you find a

promising book, check to see what "people who bought this book" also bought.

- Go to a bookstore and spend some time browsing in sections related to your problem (don't hesitate to ask the staff for help!).
- Search on Google Books, where you can read excerpts of many books for free.
- Don't limit yourself to the newest knowledge. Read the classics in the field, the books that changed how people thought, and also look for quirky little books now out of print; they can give you ideas nobody else will have.

 Stay Current

Successful creators make it a point to look back in time, but they're always alert to new developments and emerging trends. They stay on top of what's happening.

Try to get new information every day, or at a minimum every week, including

- News about world events
- New developments in your field
- What's happening in the business world
- What's new in science and technology
- New trends in art and design
- How tastes and lifestyles are changing, particularly for people much older and much younger than you

This sounds daunting, but it doesn't have to take a lot of time. You can scan magazines, surf Web sites, read just a bit below the headlines, attend local events, or glean the highlights from different fields just by circulating at a cocktail party and asking questions more engaging than "Did you try the bacon-wrapped shrimp?"

Recruit a Mentor

Exceptional creators in every field tell stories of being mentored by someone they respected, a seasoned colleague who went beyond the call of duty and took a personal interest in introducing them to the field. A study of scientists who won the Nobel Prize revealed that almost all of them had mentors, and most of their mentors also were Nobel laureates:

- John Bardeen (Nobel in Physics, 1972) was mentored by Percy Bridgman (Nobel in Physics, 1946).
- James D. Watson (Nobel in Physiology or Medicine, 1962) was mentored by Salvador Luria (Nobel in Physiology or Medicine, 1969).
- Enrico Fermi (Nobel in Physics, 1938) had *six* mentees who went on to become Nobel laureates!

A mentoring relationship is a two-way bond. Older, successful people often look for promising junior people to mentor. So once you've identified a potential mentor, don't hesitate to get in touch. Even if this individual doesn't have time, he or she will be flattered to be asked.

Famous Mentor Relationships

- Science fiction writer Isaac Asimov mentored Gene Roddenberry, creator of *Star Trek*.
- Photographer Jerome Liebling mentored Ken Burns, documentary film director and producer.
- Television reporter Barbara Walters mentored TV personality Kathy Lee Gifford.
- Russian novelist and playwright Anton Chekhov mentored the American writers Raymond Carver and Jay McInerney.

- Televangelist Billy Graham mentored Rick Warren, author of the *Purpose Driven Life*.
- Poet and editor Ezra Pound mentored poet T. S. Eliot.

The Fourth Practice of Learning: Balance Specialty with Generality

Researchers have compared the outcomes of all kinds of creativity training programs, and it turns out that the most effective programs use general creativity principles, like the ones you're learning by reading this book. Successful creativity is an ability that can be learned by anyone and applied to any field. But the research also shows that these techniques will be more effective if you've mastered a domain first, so you can apply the principles to that familiar world. That's why the first three practices—Practice Deliberately, Master Your Domain, and Learn Forever—are so essential to successful creativity. You have to know what you're talking about before you can add a new twist.

Successful creators are curious by nature. They ask questions and listen closely to the answers, even when the information has no obvious relationship to what they're working on at the moment.

As you deepen your knowledge, though, you also have to broaden it. In today's increasingly complicated world, areas of expertise are becoming more and more specialized. After ten years of learning, you risk becoming too narrowly focused—unable to communicate what you know to people of different backgrounds, unable to see how your knowledge applies to other domains. These techniques can help you balance the tension between overspecialized, zoomed-in knowledge and the big picture, the panorama that gives you perspective and puts your knowledge in context.

Be T-Shaped

Some of the most creative ideas in history have resulted from combinations of ideas from more than one area. For example, the world's first surgical robot, AESOP, came from a collaboration between a surgeon and a robotics expert. Neither would have had the necessary expertise alone—and if they hadn't been aware and open and creative enough to think outside their own area, they never would have found each other.

How can you get the benefits of specialized learning without closing yourself off to potentially exciting connections outside your area? The solution is to be *T-shaped*. This term is used by the famously creative industrial design firm IDEO to describe the sort of creative people they try to hire. The vertical bar of the *T* represents depth of expertise in one area—you won't get hired at IDEO unless you're an expert in something. But you won't get hired if you're *just* an expert, either. The horizontal bar at the top of the *T* represents a shallow, admittedly superficial awareness of a broad range of different fields. That horizontal bar is what allows you to make connections between your own expertise and potentially useful concepts and discoveries in other areas.

Branch Out

Always start with your core area of expertise—but don't stop there. Branch out and study subjects in every area that is somehow related to your problem. If you're trying to invent a better mousetrap, the most relevant knowledge would be mechanical engineering and the ability to build things with your hands. Learn about that, and then branch out:

- Read studies by animal scientists who study mouse behavior. Watch a little Walt Disney; he studied mice, too, before he drew Mickey.
- Gain a passing familiarity with home construction, to see where a home might have small gaps that mice can fit through.

- Learn a bit about food chemistry and animal nutrition, enough to understand which foods mice are drawn to and why.

Successful creators are curious by nature. They ask questions and listen closely to the answers, even when the information has no obvious relationship to what they're working on at the moment.

Helvetica

In the early 1970s Steve Jobs was a young man in search of himself. He had dropped out of Reed College, and like a lot of college dropouts he continued to hang around campus, sleeping on floors in his friends' dorm rooms. To fill his time, he would occasionally visit various classrooms at Reed, just sitting in the back—not as an official registered student. For example, he sat in on a calligraphy course, where he learned about typefaces, letter spacing, and serif and sans serif fonts. The calligraphy course had no obvious, practical value at all, but Jobs appreciated the beauty of the art form.

Ten years later, Apple was working to develop its next personal computer, the Macintosh, with its now-famous graphical user interface. Before the Mac, essentially all personal computers could only display characters in one font. But because of his calligraphy class ten years earlier, Jobs knew the beauty and creative thrill of different letterforms. He realized that the Mac's new screen technology made it possible to display multiple fonts. He insisted that the Mac's original word processor be designed to support them.

Today the entire world knows about Courier, Helvetica, and Times New Roman, and people with no training in graphics have hours of fun choosing the right font for a report or a party invitation. We owe our typographical literacy in part to a dropout's idle interest back in the 1970s.

Never turn down a chance to learn something. You never know when that knowledge might turn out to be just what you need, years later, in a changed world, for a situation you can't possibly anticipate right now.

Be a Dilettante

In 2012 the *New York Times* reported on a UCLA student, Jeremy Gleick, who has a unique habit: every day he finds time for a "learning hour"—one hour devoted to learning something new. In 2012 he passed his thousandth hour of self-study, most of it done online.

Gleick has logged every hour of learning in a spreadsheet. The topics range over the breadth of human knowledge: seventeen hours total on art history; thirty-nine on the Civil War; fourteen on weaponry; forty-one on hypnosis. He's also learned juggling, glass-blowing, banjo, and mandolin. He is, unabashedly, a "dilettante"—defined as a dabbler, an amateur, a non-professional. And he says he has yet to find a subject that isn't at least somewhat interesting to him.

iTunes U has material available for free, including full courses from MIT and Stanford that last up to thirty hours. In 2012 free classes from MIT included Philosophical Issues in Brain Science, Introduction to Algorithms, and Wheelchair Design in Developing Countries (http://web.mit.edu/itunesu). In 2012 free classes from Stanford included Colonial and Revolutionary America, How I Write, and Coding Together: Apps for iPhone and iPad (http://itunes.stanford.edu).

Or, try Coursera, with free courses from Princeton, Stanford, Caltech, and many other universities.

Dabble in something you know nothing about. Read a how-to book about a hobby you've never pursued before, such as

- Auto repair
- Woodworking
- Gardening
- Playing the harmonica
- Basket weaving

Learning is a lifelong scavenger hunt. The wonderful beauty of the creative life is that no authentic, thoughtful experience, no new glimmer of knowledge, is ever wasted.

Learn about Sufi mysticism or the Swedenborgians. Work your way through a single letter of the alphabet in an encyclopedia. Learn everything there is to know about the elbow, or tree frogs, or any other detail of the universe that catches your fancy. I will lay a wager here and now that at some point in your future, what you learn will come into play in a way you could never have predicted.

Gleick's Favorite One-Hour Learning Topics

Humanities (354 Total Hours)

- "Papyrus of Ani," *Book of the Dead* (Internet Sacred Text Archive)
- *Jazz Insights*, audio series with Gordon Vernick of Georgia State (WMLB 1690 AM)
- *History of Philosophy Without Any Gaps*, audio podcast by Peter Adamson of King's College London (iTunes U)

Science (254 Total Hours)

- A *Brief History of Time*, 1998 book by physicist Stephen Hawking

- *Introduction to Psychology*, audio lectures by Jeremy Wolfe (MIT OpenCourseWare)
- "What Technology Wants," lecture by Kevin Kelly (FORA.tv)

Skills (423 Total Hours)

- Blacksmithing class (The Crucible arts center, Oakland, California)
- "The Street Hypnotist's Handbook," steps to hypnosis by Nathan Thomas (Keys to the Mind)
- American Sign Language (ASLPro online dictionary)
- Card trick tutorials (Expert Village channel, YouTube)

 Pair Up with an Expert

Find an expert in an area that's related to your interests but unfamiliar to you. Make sure the person you choose is equally interested in what you do, and is willing to make the effort required to communicate across boundaries. Get together—at Starbucks or by Skype—at least once every month, and talk about your projects, what you've learned over the years, and what problems you're currently trying to solve.

Onward . . .

The practices in this chapter reveal the secrets of the world's most exceptional creators. These techniques show you how to invest your time to maximize your creative potential—and have fun while you're doing so. Learning is a lifelong scavenger hunt, and if you're used to quick forays for a needed fact, this approach might sound exhausting. But the wonderful beauty of the creative life is that no authentic, thoughtful experience, no new glimmer of knowledge, is ever wasted. Your brain's efficient; at some point, it will find a way to use everything you gather.

After you master the second step, learn, you're ready to soar beyond that knowledge and create something new. For that, we need the next step: look.

LOOK

How to Be Aware of the Answers All Around You

People only see what they are prepared to see.

Ralph Waldo Emerson

In 1941 George de Mestral went on a hunting trip with his dog in the Swiss Alps. It was autumn, and the underbrush prickled with burrs—a kind of seed pod that sticks to an animal's fur. This is evolution's genius: animals carry the seeds far and wide, spreading the plant's offspring over a vast area. But the mechanism is annoying for dogs—and for their owners. Burrs were stuck all over de Mestral's dog, and also on his pants. Most dog owners never notice how cleverly burrs are designed; they just get annoyed when they bloody their fingers trying to remove them.

De Mestral was annoyed, too. But unlike decades of previous dog owners, he was also intrigued. He saved one of the burrs and looked at it closely under a microscope. At the end of each of its sharp spines, he noticed a tiny hook. These hooks snagged on fur and clothing, allowing the burr to hang on and travel.

Looking closely gave de Mestral an idea: if he could put spines with hooks on one side and tiny loops on the other, he could make a new kind of fastener, an improved version of the zipper. The result? Velcro. De Mestral retired as a multimillionaire.

Now let's switch to a failure that zig zagged into a success. Hasbro came up with a lollipop that played a song when you licked it. The trick was a newly invented technology that let a tune resonate through the teeth and jawbone. Alas, the singing lollipop cost ten dollars, and no self-respecting parent was going to spend that much for a piece of candy. The lollipop was a flop.

A few years later, around 2000, another team at Hasbro was trying to develop a new child's toothbrush, and they needed a gimmick. Someone looked in the "dead ideas" file and found the lollipop. The second team put the technology into the toothbrush, and had it play a two-minute song as long as it was touching the teeth—thereby making sure a child would brush for at least two minutes, the minimum recommended by dentists. Parents gladly paid ten dollars for healthy teeth, and the toothbrush was a singing success.

A final zig zag example. More than a century ago, two sisters—Mildred and Patty Hill—composed a song they titled "Good Morning to You." Nobody bought it. The sisters kept tinkering, though, trying different lyrics until they arrived at a version that was just right. You've sung it countless times: it's called "Happy Birthday to You."

These three examples are very different, but they have one important element in common: the discipline of looking. Simply by seeing the same thing in a new way, these inventors came up with ideas that resonated with millions of people.

How *do* we see? It seems obvious: the eyes scan the environment, a photographic image is projected onto the retina, and then that image is passed on to the brain. But this simple account is wrong, because seeing is as much about the brain as it is about the eye.

Rodolfo Llinas, a neuroscientist at NYU School of Medicine, says that what we see is, in large part, a projection created by our brain. Scientists used to think that visual information from our eyes was processed upward, from the eye to the visual cortex, and then on to the higher brain regions that are responsible for thinking and creativity. But recent studies indicate something very different: thousands of neurons are sending information from the higher brain regions back into the visual cortex.

By Llinas's estimate, only 20 percent of our perceptions are based on information coming from the outside world; the other 80 percent, our mind fills in. Neuroscientists don't yet fully understand exactly how the different pathways intersect to create what we see. But Llinas makes a surprising claim: that there is no essential difference between waking and sleeping. In both states, our brain actively constructs our view of the world.

> The question is not what you look at, but what you see.
>
> *Henry David Thoreau*

Professor David Perkins of Harvard studied poets and painters while they were doing creative work. As they critically examined their own work in progress, they demonstrated an almost uncanny ability to notice problems, difficulties, and opportunities. This "noticing" then guided the next stage of their work, as they refined and improved what they'd done. In other words, much of their creative brilliance came from their ability to look at their work in just the right way.

Want to see how your mind's ability to notice things plays a role in creativity? Take out a watch with a second hand, grab paper and a pencil to write down your times, and try the these three exercises.

First, look through the following letters as fast as you can, and count the number of *x*'s. Write down how long it took you to count the *x*'s.

q	r	x	t	b	f	x	m	g	n	x	z
c	f	l	q	x	b	m	s	y	z	u	v
h	x	g	p	s	t	b	h	x	f	t	l
m	r	b	x	p	s	l	m	r	f	x	b
q	p	l	f	z	x	p	t	o	l	f	s
l	x	r	x	f	s	l	z	x	m	r	p

1 2

14 sec

Second, look through the same block of letters, but this time, find any of the five letters *r*, *x*, *v*, *s*, and *w*—and not by looking through five separate times, but with just one scan. Write down your time again.

22 sec

That's harder, but it doesn't take five times as long. That's because your mind has an amazing ability to create new categories that help you complete tasks. Psychologists have discovered that with enough practice, you can scan for a large set of targets almost as fast as you scan for just one. To see what I mean, try the third exercise: go to the group of letters that follows and scan for any of the five letters *a*, *e*, *i*, *o*, and *u*. Write down how long it takes.

q	m	w	n	e	b	r	v	t	c	y	x
u	z	i	l	o	k	p	j	a	h	s	g
d	f	q	m	w	n	e	b	r	v	t	c
y	x	u	z	i	l	o	k	p	j	a	h
s	g	d	f	q	m	w	n	e	b	r	v
t	c	y	x	u	z	i	l	o	k	p	j

10 sec

Almost everyone finishes the vowel search much faster than the *r*, *x*, *v*, *s*, *w* search. In fact, many people can do this just as fast as looking only for *x*'s. That's because our past experience and learning change the way we see. We don't need to keep checking our list, because we memorized those vowels back in first grade.

(By the way, there are twelve *x*'s; twenty-three instances of *r*, *x*, *v*, *s*, and *w*; and fourteen vowels.)

In the last chapter, we talked about the huge role learning plays in successful creativity. Trained noticing is a form of learning, and it can speed up many processes. But the flip side of trained noticing is that it can also block you from seeing unexpected and surprising things. And it's those unexpected, random associations that often spark truly creative ideas.

So how do you free your well-trained mind to make unexpected associations? You go *beyond* your training and expertise by mastering the discipline of looking. Creative people are very good at finding exactly what they need to see to take the next creative step forward. Throughout the day, whether they're shopping for groceries or fixing a meal for their children, successful creators often notice possible paths to a solution. That's because their eyes are prepared to see potential solutions everywhere they look.

Psychologists are beginning to understand just how this creative seeing works. When you're working hard on a problem and then get stumped, you're left with what are called "failure indices"—stored memories of exactly where you were when you got stumped. These bookmarks keep your subconscious mind attuned to any potential solution. So first, you need to think about a problem until you get stumped. Second, set the problem aside, and trust that the lingering failure index will stay active in your subconscious mind. Then, most important of all, you need to look in a new way, to notice examples or bits of inspiration in your environment that can reactivate your failure index and move you past the block.

Here's an example. For my son, Graham's, ninth birthday, my wife and I gave him a huge airplane made of Styrofoam. It was over four feet long and had a wingspan just as large. The first time he took it outside to play, he broke the fuselage in half. (Like I didn't see that coming!) We tried to glue it back together, but no glue was strong enough, and it kept breaking right in the same spot. Graham was crushed. I was stumped. How could I fix this airplane?

The next week, at a conference, I was eating appetizers at an evening reception. While I was enjoying little cubes of cheese on toothpicks, suddenly my airplane failure index came to life: I realized I could take a couple of toothpicks and stick them into the center of the Styrofoam fuselage right across the break, to hold the two broken pieces in place. After the reception, I rushed home to try it. I inserted two toothpicks halfway into one of the broken pieces; then I added glue, and I lined up and squeezed the other broken piece onto the two exposed toothpick ends. It worked like a charm!

The way you look at the world determines how creative you can be. By looking more closely, more patiently, or from a different angle, you realize how your brain has shaped your previous perceptions and guided (or limited) your thinking. Once you understand how your mind and vision influence each other, you can begin to see the world afresh.

The Practices

When you've mastered the discipline of looking, you are constantly, quietly aware. You don't just see what you expect to see. You see the new, the unusual, the surprising. You see what others take for granted, and what they incorrectly assume. You are directly connected to your senses, so you perceive clearly and accurately. You expose yourself to new experiences eagerly, without hesitation; you regularly seek out new stimuli, new situations, and new information. You're constantly expanding your personal library of sights and sounds, behaviors and reactions, needs and wants.

The way you look at the world determines how creative you can be.

I named this step look because our world is so visual now, but it also includes listening, and any other way of observing the world around you. To turn this open attention into creativity, you need to master three practices: Use Fresh Eyes, Grab New Sights and Cool Sounds, and Render It Visible.

The First Practice of Looking: Use Fresh Eyes

Use this practice if you're feeling stumped. You're stuck in a rut or spinning your wheels, your thoughts as trite as the clichés that describe them. You keep thinking of the same old solutions, the ones you already know don't work.

Using fresh eyes teaches you how to look at the world the way the most excep-tional creators do. You begin to observe exactly what will move you forward on your creative journey. You find answers to your bookmarked failure indices, and the new ideas propel you forward, right over your writer's block or techni-cal snag. Best of all, you recognize when your ways of seeing are part of the problem. You open your eyes a little wider and look beyond familiar, established patterns.

> I love life, I live it trying to observe carefully everything I see. I examine it by touch, I watch it, and I observe every small thing about it.
>
> *Albert Szent-Györgyi, winner of the 1937 Nobel Prize in Physiology or Medicine*

 Become More Aware

> Mindfulness is simply the process of noticing new things . . . To be a true artist is to be mindful.
>
> **Ellen Langer**

Professor Ellen Langer of Harvard studies what she calls *mindfulness*, a state of active observation. Back in the 1970s she started noticing how often people do things without thinking. This "mindlessness" is an efficient way to get through the day: we shower the same way every morning; we drive the same route to work every day; and many of our work tasks are repetitive, so our brain can offload them to the unconscious mind. But mindlessness stops being efficient the minute something changes. When the regular routine no longer works, we fail.

You saw at the beginning of this chapter how knowing about vowels made a search task much easier. But sometimes these same mental categories lead to mindlessness. Without thinking, we plop new perceptions into old categories—forcing the new information to fit our expectations rather than using it to create new categories.

For example, many of us find a way to immediately categorize people we meet. Was that a Southern accent? Are they from our town, or somewhere else? Professional, graduate degree, blue collar? Where did they go to high school or college?

We're quick to do this with political or economic opinions— especially if we consider ourselves knowledgeable about politics. We hear one sentence and decide the person's "liberal" or "conservative." We're often so busy assigning the label, we fail to hear what that individual is really saying.

How can we smash those rigid mental categories? By cultivating mindfulness, Langer says. She's identified four ways:

- Have an open and curious attitude.
- Interact with the world around you, and pay lively attention to changes in your environment.
- Actively create new categories rather than relying on existing, stereotypical categories.
- Look at your experiences from multiple perspectives, and use feedback to adapt behavior.

Langer believes that what distinguishes artists from others is their mindful state. You'll notice—if, that is, you're looking!—that many of the techniques in this chapter echo her work on mindfulness. For greater creativity, you have to stop living on autopilot and start paying attention.

Make Your Own Luck

Professor Richard Wiseman studied two groups of people. The first group described themselves as "exceptionally lucky"; the second group said they were extremely *unlucky*. What, he wondered, is the difference between lucky and unlucky people? Is there a way to make your own luck?

Wiseman found that there is. And one of the most important ways to increase your luck is by looking. Lucky people pay more attention to what's going on around them. They're also more open to opportunities that come along spontaneously. The unlucky people Wiseman studied were just the opposite: they were stuck in routine patterns, and so focused on their narrow goals that they failed to notice unexpected opportunities.

In one experiment, Wiseman gave both lucky and unlucky people a newspaper, and told them to look through it and tell him how many photographs were inside. On average, the unlucky people took about two minutes to count the photos. The lucky people took just a few seconds. How were they so fast? Because on the second page of the newspaper, Wiseman had the printer insert the words "Stop counting—there are 43 photographs in this newspaper" in very large type that took up half the page. The unlucky people tended to miss it, and the lucky people tended to see it.

How could unlucky people not notice this huge, half-page message? They had defined their goal so tightly—"I am looking for pictures"—that they didn't see any text. Unlucky people miss opportunities because they're too focused on looking for something else. Lucky people don't fixate; they're skilled at creating, noticing, and acting on unexpected opportunities. The phrase "carpe diem" was invented for them—they seize the day, and any possibility it holds.

Lucky people also have two other characteristics. First, they talk to lots of people; they're always networking with others. Not with a specific, self-serving agenda, mind you; their sort of networking is usually unselfconscious, done purely for the fun of learning about other people's experiences.

Liven Up the Party

One lucky person told Wiseman about a special technique he'd developed to force him to meet different types of people. He'd noticed that at social events he tended to always talk to people similar to him. So to stop himself from that natural tendency, before he arrives at a party he thinks of a color, and then he decides to only talk to people who are wearing that color.

Or try this: before going to a party where you'll meet new people, decide not to use your usual, tired opener: "Where are you from?" "What do you do?" Try something different, something that connects to the occasion or environment and reveals a new dimension of the person you're talking to. There will be all sorts of possibilities, depending on where you are:

- "Have you ever traveled overseas?"
- "Are you close to anyone who's in the military?"
- "How did you meet your spouse?"

Second, lucky people tend to have a more relaxed attitude toward life—when they encounter bad luck, their relaxed attitude helps them turn it into good luck. Unlucky people are more tense and anxious, Wiseman discovered, and that anxiety prevents them from noticing unexpected things. Because lucky people are relaxed, they observe more, and they reinterpret even negative events as positive opportunities.

The good news is that it's easy to change your luck. Wiseman has created a "luck school," a one-month set of activities that teaches the practices associated with lucky people. After one month of training, 80 percent of his students said they had become much luckier!

Look for New Patterns

David Perkins's research shows how easy it is for us to create new categories—like r, x, v, s, w—and almost immediately use those categories to change the way we think. The following technique will exercise this ability, and it just might get you out in front of the latest new trend or social change.

What you're going to do is look for patterns where you wouldn't normally look for them. Take advantage of situations where you might otherwise be bored, or deep in a familiar routine:

- Waiting in the doctor's office, why not thumb through that stack of dated magazines, and look for trends in the graphic design of magazine covers?

- Stuck in traffic and listening to the radio, what trends do you notice in popular music?

- When you're shopping, look for trends in product packaging.

- Instead of surfing away from TV commercials, why not think about how they're changing over the years (the music, the speed of the edits, the words) and ask yourself why?

- Before you toss your junk mail every day, skim through it. Or, save it and flip through the pile at the end of each month. Look for trends in marketing, in values, and in what fears or desires sellers hope to tap.

- When driving, notice when three lanes merge down to two, or which highway exits are cloverleafs or instead have a single exit leading to a stoplight, and see if you can figure out why.

Cultivate Your Senses

See, hear, and taste with greater sensitivity and discrimination. Listen to inflections in the conversations around you and see how much you can intuit about the speakers' various emotional states. Taste a complicated new dish and try to identify every ingredient. Enter a room and notice where the lights are and how they affect the room's mood.

This technique is particularly good for enhancing your aesthetic judgment. Put yourself into an experience that you don't know much about:

- Visit an art museum.
- Attend a wine tasting.
- Listen to a jazz solo.
- Listen to a classical music station on the radio.

These are all fairly high-class activities, but you can do the same thing with more mainstream art forms. The key is to pick something that's very different from what you're used to. If you're already knowledgeable about art, wine, jazz, and classical music, then choose from the following list:

- Listen to a hip-hop or rap artist and try to figure out the rhyme patterns.
- Watch a Sunday morning children's cartoon and put yourself in the shoes of the animators—what decisions were they making as they created this?
- Stop by a fast-food restaurant you've never been to before. Before you order, look through the entire menu: all the item descriptions, the prices, the special combinations. What do you think is the target market? What's the strategy?
- Listen to a country music station on the radio.

At first, everything will be unfamiliar, and you won't know enough to judge the quality—or even to notice what's going on. It's important to embrace and welcome that feeling of unfamiliarity. Instead of letting it unsettle you or just deciding you don't like it, make an effort to figure out what's at play. What makes this work aesthetical? What knowledge would it take to make you an expert in this field?

Practice Ethnography

Ethnography is the approach anthropologists use to study another culture. It's the art of noticing ways of life in a particular culture that its people aren't consciously aware of, yet that they practice consistently, unthinkingly.

When you're an outsider, you naturally notice details that locals take for granted. The first time I left the United States, in 1988, I traveled to Paris on vacation. When I shopped, I was surprised to notice that every item was priced with an even number: 4.00 francs, or 20.00 francs (this was long before the Euro currency had been created). Tax was already included, so you never got back a handful of change. No Parisian would think anything of it, but I did—because in the United States, items are usually priced to end in 99 cents ($3.99 or $19.99), and tax is added, so every purchase is an odd number of cents and you always receive a handful of change.

It's relatively easy to notice differences in another country. But you can also train yourself to see familiar surroundings in this way. For readers in the United States, ask yourself: "Why do we have cheerleaders at sporting events?" "Why is it an accepted practice to hire a lawyer to 'fix' a speeding ticket, at the same time that bribes are illegal?" "Why do waiters introduce themselves by name, as if they intend to start a friendship?"

Look for Serendipity

"Luck," it's said, "is when preparation meets opportunity." Well, creativity happens when preparation meets a surprise.

The word "serendipity" means "happy accident"; it refers to the coincidence of finding something good or useful without looking for it. The word has a pretty strange history. The English writer Horace Walpole coined it after reading an old Persian fairy tale, "The Three Princes of Serendip," because, he said, the three heroes "were always making discoveries, by accidents and sagacity, of things which they were not in quest of."

A man of genius makes no mistakes; his errors are the portals of discovery.

James Joyce

Be alert to valuable accidents. Without training yourself to look, you might just become annoyed by something unexpected and brush past it in a single-minded pursuit of your goal.

Many inventions have resulted from looking closely at accidents:

- The float process for making glass (while washing dishes, Sir Alistair Pilkington saw a film of soap form)
- Penicillin (Sir Alexander Fleming accidentally contaminated a laboratory bacterial culture with mold)
- Saccharin (in 1879 chemist Constantine Fahlberg noticed that his hand tasted sweet after working on coal tar derivatives)
- The Slinky toy (Richard and Betty James based it on a failed World War II military tension spring experiment)
- The microwave oven (the cooking potential of microwaves was first discovered when a radar prototype accidentally melted a nearby candy bar)
- Chewing gum (this was invented during an attempt to make a rubber substitute from chicle trees)

Langer did an experiment in which she simply asked people to draw a picture. The twist was, she secretly caused an accident that forced each person to make a mistake while drawing. Half of the people had been told in advance, "It is human to make a mistake ... just incorporate it into your drawing." Many of these people in fact did incorporate the mistake into what they were doing and kept drawing, and their sketches ended up being much more creative than those of the people who did not get this instruction. The point of the experiment? That it's pretty easy to change the way you think about mistakes.

Remember, unlucky people focus narrowly on their goal; lucky people work toward their goal but stay open to the unexpected. It's important to avoid making an overly specific, rigid plan ahead of time. If you're too fixed on where you think you're going, then you'll perceive an accident as an annoyance, and your first instinct will be to work around it. Start your work without too detailed a plan; expect valuable accidents to happen.

There's a tension here with the first step, ask, which is all about the importance of having a good question and a clear goal. Your goal must be clear, but it must stay general, because the greatest creativity happens when the goal isn't too detailed and specific. The most creative problems provide a general guide forward, yet leave room for improvisations in response to mistakes and surprises.

Spot the Spandrels

In architecture, a spandrel is the space at the top of an arched doorway. Spandrels are a necessary byproduct of putting an arched opening into a rectangular wall. More generally, a spandrel is any space that exists not by design, but as a necessary side effect of something else. Here are a couple I've noticed:

- The strip of grass between the airport parking garage and the taxi pickup lane
- The bit of floor between your toilet and the wall behind it

Come to think of it, these places always seem to either collect dirt or make ideal locations for shrubbery! Challenge yourself to find one tomorrow, and figure out why it's there. What design or architectural decisions caused it to be? Could you change something to get rid of it?

Switch Perspectives

Try to perceive things from a different perspective.

- As you walk down the street, imagine yourself sitting in a wheelchair. How would the world look different? What would you be more likely to notice—cracks in the sidewalk? Ramps up the curbs?
- Imagine yourself as a child four feet tall—how would grown-ups look different? What would you notice more?
- In an art gallery, sit down on the floor to see how Pablo Picasso's work would look to a toddler.

Take a problem you're trying to solve. How would you see and think differently about this problem if you were . . .

- A lawyer?
- A sculptor?
- A journalist?
- An electrician?
- An actor?

This technique sometimes works better if you can think of a specific person, like the actor Brad Pitt; the journalist Anderson Cooper; or your uncle Harry, who's a master electrician.

The Second Practice of Looking: Grab New Sights and Cool Sounds

Use these techniques if you're looking for some new image or object that will push you past an impasse and get you back on the path to creativity. These techniques help make that next zig zag possible.

This second practice shows you how to seek out new things to see, thereby creating more opportunities for unexpected connections, one of the most powerful sources of creativity. Because the first practice is more basic, it's best to start there. Mastering the first practice gets you up to the level of successful creators. But if you've mastered the first practice and you're still stumped, turn to this second practice—a series of advanced techniques that exceptional creators and artists use every day.

Start Tripping

Take a trip—to the zoo, train station, natural history museum, hobby and craft shop—anyplace, really, as long as it's crammed with physical objects.

Go to a yard sale or an antique store. Browse slowly; pay close attention even to the items that you'd never consider buying, those that you don't find very interesting. *Why* aren't they interesting? Be specific. Is it the material they're made of? Their shape, size, or color? Their fussiness or ordinariness? Their intended use?

Take a trip to a high-end mall, its expensive shops filled with the latest luxe styles. You're not looking to buy; you're looking for inspiration. What's surprising? What's really new? What makes you laugh?

Go to a trade show for an industry you know nothing about. As I write this, I live in the Midwest, near a lot of large farms, and one of my favorite trade shows focuses on farm equipment and seeds—something quite distant from my psychology research!

A trip works even better with a group. When you're done, talk about what you noticed and try to force connections between what you've seen and the problem you're hoping to solve.

Relax and Listen

I've studied theatrical improv and played jazz, and those are interesting experiences, because when improvising, you have to act without knowing what your action means. When you improvise a line of dialogue, you don't know how it's going to be interpreted and where the scene will zig or zag. When you point up at the sky and say, "Did you see that?" your partner gets to decide what it is you actually saw—you won't know until you hear your partner's response. You have to trust the rest of the ensemble to catch what you toss.

Once you're good at improvisation, you get a special thrill from watching what somebody else does with what you've thrown out there. But for a novice, the uncertainty can be nerve-racking. I started taking classical piano lessons at the age of ten, and by high school I was good enough to play with the school choir and in the annual musical theater show—reading from a musical score, of course, and after lots of practice playing through each score over and over. One day, one of my friends told me that our high school's eighteen-piece big band jazz ensemble needed a pianist, and that I should play with them! I got pretty excited, but I didn't know anything about jazz. My first time in rehearsal, the band director handed me sheet music that wasn't like anything I'd seen before. There were *no notes on the page!* There were only harmonic chord symbols, and I had no idea what they meant. I learned very quickly that I was expected to create my own notes, within the loose structure provided by the chord symbols. And on top of that, I was supposed to listen to the other musicians while I played, and to make sure that what I was improvising aligned with the parts *they* were improvising. For a classical pianist like me, this seemed almost impossible. There was just no way I could listen and respond in an intelligent way to a new rhythmic pattern the drummer was playing; it was all I could do to figure out where my own fingers were going to go.

It took me the first year just to learn how to improvise my own parts. And then, soon after that, I gradually learned how to listen to what everybody else was doing. If the drummer hit the snare drum off-beat, then in the next measure I might play my chord off-beat in the same way—*zig*. And everyone in the band would hear our tiny interaction and then *zag* in a new direction with something else interesting, because that's just the way jazz is.

Whatever your field, improvise a little.

Play with Children's Toys

Back in the early 1980s, when I worked at a company that designed many of Atari's hit video games, we game designers all kept the latest wind-up toys on our desks. Even though I stopped designing video games long ago, I still keep as many toys on my desk as will fit, and I often take a handful into meetings. My favorites from the 1980s are clear plastic cubes made by Tomy, three inches on each side, which have miniature arcade games inside. (For example, when you wind one of them up, the basket inside starts moving from side to side, and you have to use a tiny lever to shoot equally tiny metal balls into the basket while it's in motion.) I'm not the least bit self-conscious about my toy collection: if you walk into just about any supercreative company, you'll find toys all over the place. If you have young children, you've no doubt already got a pile of toys lying around that they no longer play with; if you don't, go spend fifty dollars and buy yourself a collection.

Children at play are geniuses at making surprising new connections, and creativity comes from the zigs and zags that result. When children play, they constantly experiment with every object to see how it might combine with other objects. They combine marbles and spinner tops to invent a new game, for instance. When my son, Graham, was eight years old, he took the brightly colored

You can find great toys for adults at www.fatbraintoys.com and www.officeplayground.com.

disks from a donut-themed game and combined them with small magnets to create a new game. (He never once played the donut game itself!)

So don't just play with the toy in the way it's designed. Be like a child: try out new ways of playing, new ways of combining toys to invent your own game. Playfulness isn't silly at all; it helps us reach more creative solutions.

Shape Your Day

Wiseman found that lucky people are more likely to notice unexpected things. But he noticed something else, too: lucky people make a conscious effort to introduce change into their lives, or to put themselves in situations in which they're more likely to see something unexpected.

Encounter the unexpected:

- Listen to a different radio station each day.
- Take a different route to work.
- Shop at a different grocery store every week.

In the morning, select a basic geometric shape: a circle, triangle, or square (or even a zig zag!). Let's say you select a square. Consciously focus on finding instances of that shape throughout your day, and try to make connections between those objects and the challenge you face. As you drive to work, you might see a street sign that's square. In the office, some of the pictures on the wall might be squares. Look for square patterns in the carpets you're walking on. Force yourself to connect these shapes to your creative challenge, no matter how far you have to reach to do so. (That wild, long reach is part of the point; creativity's not supposed to be obvious.)

Remember to Look at Bad Examples

This technique will sound crazy, but it's a great way to get your confidence up. Read some purple prose, *really* bad writing.

Wince over lurid paintings, preferably on velvet, or a stack of blurry, poorly cropped photographs. Examine some gadget that's awkwardly engineered and bound to break the first time you use it.

Normally it's best to look at the finest examples in your creative domain, but every once in a while looking at a few that are really awful will erase any insecurities that are still plaguing you. You know you can do better, and the ideas start flowing right away.

Flip Through Strange Magazines

Buy a magazine you would normally never read, one that's far removed from any of your interests. There are hunting magazines, hot rod magazines, and magazines for writers and for artists. If you're a man, buy *Cosmopolitan* or *Elle*. If you're afraid of getting anywhere near a body of water, buy *Sailing* magazine. Buy the tattoo magazine *Skin and Ink*; or buy *Guitar World*, a magazine for professional and amateur guitarists.

The product design firm IDEO has office subscriptions to over a hundred magazines, and they're kept out where everyone can dabble when they need an idea.

Business writer Tom Peters says that whenever he's at the airport about to board a plane, he buys as many as fifteen different magazines from the newsstand. Then, on the plane, he skims through them quickly, waiting for that moment of surprise and connection. When something strikes a chord, he tears out the page and saves it to study back in his office.

Absorb New Media

If you read the *New York Times* every morning, try reading the colorful *New York Post* for a couple of days. If you read the *National Enquirer*, switch to the *Wall Street Journal*.

Listen to NPR or your city's most popular pop-rock station, whichever you'd normally not hear. If you're really feeling brave, turn the dial to talk radio you don't agree with.

Watch a different TV news channel.

Browse the *Huffington Post* or Drudge Report online.

Read, listen to, or watch this new media with the eyes of an editor: How is the selection of stories different from what you're used to? What about the tone of the language? Are the advertisements different? Try to explain why—is this done to respond to a different readership? A different editorial mission? Look closely for the subtle ways in which this new media alternative is different from your regular source of information. Don't just look for differences that reinforce your existing prejudices; look for new insights.

The next time you're in a bookstore, make sure to walk through a section you never visit. Skim the titles, look through some tables of contents, read the back covers.

If you want a new book, don't just read it online with Google Books or download it to your e-reader. Go to a library, go to the shelf, and find the book. Then spend a minute or two scanning the titles of all of the books on the same shelf and on the shelf above and on the shelf below. Countless researchers throughout history have told stories of going to find a particular book, and then happening on another one right next to it that they never knew existed . . . and that contained the answer they were seeking.

Go Walkabout

Walk around your neighborhood as though you're on your own private scavenger hunt. Pay close attention to the slight rises and dips in the street, gentle enough that you'd normally not notice them—but that you'd feel if you were using a wheelchair. Look at every chimney. Is it on the left or right side of the house? Why isn't it at the front or back? Is it brick? What color is it? How many chimneys are there for each house?

> Not all those who wander are lost.
>
> J.R.R. Tolkien

A few years back the wooden front door of our old house rotted completely through, and rain started leaking in. We needed a new door, fast. I quickly learned that there are a huge number of options for new doors, and I had no idea what I wanted. I walked around my neighborhood and looked at every door—*seeing* it for the first time. Did it have a storm door? Did it have a window? Were the panes separated by black or brass? I knew I would have to go home, thumb through a gigantic catalog, and choose from among hundreds of options. Gradually the choice became clear: I didn't want a storm door, because it covered up the artful window design, and I didn't want windows that were easy to see through, because I cherish my family's privacy. I also noticed that a lot of doors were the same color as the window shutters—but some weren't—and I liked the different ones better. After logging all those miles, the choices came easily, and I even thought up some creative modifications that never would have occurred to me. The result? We have a door that's not like any other door in our neighborhood—but that could never have happened without my looking at the other doors first.

If you live in a city, there's a lot more going on for you to notice. So take advantage of it. Go for a walk down a busy sidewalk—and make sure you're not in a hurry. Notice kids playing hopscotch, an elderly guy

> Research shows that Japanese people seek out a bustling, busy environment when they're thinking about ideas, whereas Europeans prefer to be alone. In this case, try to be more like the Japanese!

smoking a cigar at a newsstand, a schnauzer glaring at a Great Dane. Take about five times longer than you normally would; stop occasionally, pause in a doorway or lean against a parking meter, and take a few seconds to absorb the passing scene.

As you're walking, look for objects, situations, or events that you can connect to the problem you're hoping to solve. Take a notepad or a digital voice recorder with you, and keep a list. When you get back home, examine each item on your list and look for additional connections.

Travel

Traveling is a time-tested way to enhance your ability to see. The key is to go somewhere noticeably different from where you live.

> One's destination is never a place, but rather a new way of looking at things.
>
> *Henry Miller*

Paris? Bangkok? Sure, if you have the time and money. But if you can't afford to travel the world right now, that doesn't mean you can't go to a new place. Just travel a few hours to a very different town or city. I live in a big city, and I often take day trips to small country towns.

Multinationals Are More Creative

Researchers have found that people who have lived in more than one country—multinationals, biculturals, immigrants—are more creative. Maybe it's because they become masters at looking. Their experience makes them expert ethnographers; they know how fluid people's language, values, beliefs, and rituals can be. If you're a student, and you have an opportunity for a semester or a year in another country, take it. If you're moving up in an organization and you're offered a stint overseas, take it. Time spent in another country will pay dividends for a lifetime when it comes to your ability to see and perceive creatively.

The Third Practice of Looking: Render It Visible

Use these techniques to translate what you see into creative action. Creative people don't just notice things; they notice, and then they act. They immediately jot down or record what they've observed, and their mind begins working with it.

The techniques of the second practice help get you into situations where you'll see new sights. The third practice's techniques help you act on what you've seen, instead of keeping it tucked inside your head or letting it float away again. By externalizing and expressing it, you move directly into creativity. You'll start to see more clearly, once you get used to describing what you're seeing. And when you become skilled at looking, you'll see so much every day that if you don't keep a record, you'll forget most of it.

The techniques that follow are used by artists and creators in just about every profession.

Keep an Idea Log

Children's author Judy Blume always keeps a notebook with ideas that don't fit the section she's currently working on: ideas for names of characters, descriptive details of scenes, bits of dialogue. "I keep things I don't want to lose," she explains. Writer Thomas Mann did the same, keeping "scribbled notes, memory props, external details, colorful odds and ends, psychological formulations, fragmentary inspirations." Now Pinterest lets you save electronic images that inspire you, too—and peek at other people's electronic scrapbooks.

Keep a notebook, sketchbook, iPad, or voice memo recorder with you at all times, and write down, draw, or record anything you notice that interests you. This kind of notebook, whether paper or digital, is sometimes called a "seed file" because it contains seeds that might one day grow into successful creativity. Use your notebook to keep all of the ideas that seem somehow to have potential, even though you don't yet know exactly how.

Famous creators who kept notebooks include Thomas Edison; Benjamin Franklin; Leonardo da Vinci (seven thousand pages exist, and scholars estimate that this is just half of what he left when he died); the Wright brothers; Virginia Woolf; Carl Jung; and Charles Darwin.

Go back to your notebook every three or six months and skim through it. Each time, you'll see your old notes differently, through the eyes of your current situation. And more often than you'd think, one of those old notes or sketches will be just what you need to move forward on your creative path.

Start an Idea Box

Collect a box of interesting things. It's best if they're small and inexpensive. One of your child's broken old toys, for example, or a piece of odd-shaped wood you found lying next to a construction site. My own box contains a metal nutcracker; a pillbox with seven compartments, one for each day of the week; and a bunch of strange items from the hardware store, like replacement faucet handles and a piece of large pipe.

The idea box is a three-dimensional version of the idea log, and it serves the same purpose: to store interesting sights and objects so that you can look back at them later, from a different perspective.

It's best to collect small things, because you'll eventually have quite a few items, and you'll use the idea box more if you can take it with you to a meeting or a brainstorming session.

Just thinking about what might be good to put in my box has helped me look in a new way—when I'm at the hobby or craft store or the hardware store, or even when I come across a pile of old junk. I've created a new category for myself: "things that would be interesting to have in my idea box."

Set a Google Alert

Sign up for Google Alerts on a phrase related to your problem. It's free, and Google sends you a daily e-mail with all of the Web pages that have used that phrase each day. You have to define your problem carefully, because if you choose something too broad—like "career advancement" or "finding a mate"—you'll get thousands of hits every day. Try to narrow your phrase enough that you get no more than ten hits each day, so it stays relevant and doesn't become overwhelming.

Create a Personal Hall of Fame

Your personal hall of fame is a group of famous people you like and respect. It should have at least ten people; and make sure they're from all different walks of life, not a single profession.

When you face a creative challenge, use an Internet search to find famous quotations from these ten people that are connected to your challenge. There are tons of Web sites that collect such quotations; just pick one from each hall of famer. Then group them all together—maybe cut and paste them into a word processing document—and look for connections. Sit for at least five minutes and think about ways the quotes combine, themes that run through all of them, unexpected juxtapositions and what they might mean. See if this cross-fertilization prompts a new idea related to your challenge.

Appoint a Personal Board of Directors

The personal board of directors is similar to your hall of fame, but this time the people should be the most successful individuals in your own field, the ones you'd love to talk to about your problem. Select about five. Do some research about them, and read at least a little bit of biographical information about each person. Post photos of them on the wall as an inspiration. When you read stories about them, pay close attention to how they ask questions and solve problems, and what daily practices they use.

Onward . . .

Now you've learned about the three practices that successful creators use to observe the world. When you master the discipline of looking, you begin to see in ways that move your creative process forward. You'll find yourself returning to the techniques in this chapter, because looking is so essential to the entire creative process. It can help you identify good problems (ask) and help you come up with great ideas (think).

Now we continue our journey with the fourth step. Everything you've done in the first three steps prepares your mind to begin working on creative solutions. The fourth step, play, happens when your mind takes advantage of all of that effort and works its magic, bringing together different ideas, memories, and images to generate surprising new solutions.

PLAY

How to Free Your Mind to Imagine Possible Worlds

> Almost all really new ideas have a certain aspect of foolishness when they are first produced.
>
> **Alfred N. Whitehead, philosopher**

For many of us, text messaging is like breathing—necessary, automatic, and reflexive. It hasn't been around very long, though: it's based on Short Message Service (SMS), a technology that's only been available on cell phones since the early 1990s. When SMS was first invented by the Dutch company CMG, it was designed to be used strictly for internal maintenance purposes. For example, CMG used it to broadcast messages to its customers about network problems, and to notify them if they had a voice message.

CMG had no plans for customers to send messages to each other, but amateur hackers in Europe, playing around with their phones, somehow stumbled on a way to do it. Then, to their delight, they discovered that this new pirated messaging system was free! The phone companies hadn't designed any way to track usage. Word spread fast; before long, teenagers across Europe—who often bought prepaid mobile phones—all knew that every text message was free. Suddenly, millions of messages were flying back and forth every month, and phone companies were scrambling to figure out how to bill per message.

Text messaging, now the norm, was not a corporate invention dreamed up in a research lab. It emerged from the zigs and zags of play and exploration.

Because text messaging was designed for internal phone company use only, prior to 1999 you could only send text messages to friends who used the same carrier network.

There's an intimate connection between play and creativity—why?

- Play is when you let your mind wander. You put aside the hard work of the first three steps, you relax, and you give your subconscious time to work its magic.

- Play is when you enter the province of the imagination. Instead of dealing in precut, dry, dusty old facts, you envision what's possible. You create alternate worlds, making them more colorful and interesting, smarter and more meaningful, than the current reality.

Children are naturally creative. They experiment tirelessly, combining things that aren't supposed to go together—marbles and Play-Doh, race cars and bouncy balls. They paint purple grass and give trees arms; they dress penguins in top hats; and they never, ever fear looking fool-

Did you ever hear a small boy complain of having to hang about a railway station and wait for a train? No; for him to be inside a railway station is to be inside a cavern of wonder.

G. K. *Chesterton*

ish. They let their minds wander freely, and they visualize the ridiculous so well, it's often clever.

At the 2008 Art Center Design Conference, Tim Brown, the head of IDEO, gave the audience members thirty seconds to draw the person sitting next to them. You could hear the giggles, groans, and apologies as they sketched. Afterward, Brown pointed out that children, given the same task, show no embarrassment whatsoever. They happily show their masterpiece to their model, because they haven't learned to fear judgment. And fear is what inhibits creativity, making us conservative in our thinking and timid in our execution.

The techniques in this chapter help you summon back that childlike instinct to toy with the world, to pretend, to try on exotic costumes and turn everyday objects into props and cardboard boxes into a kingdom.

> To make films is also to plunge again by its deepest roots down to the world of childhood.
>
> *Ingmar Bergman, film director*

Adult life is filled with pressure and deadlines. To create the space for imagination, dreaming, and insight, it is your solemn *duty* to master the discipline of playing.

The boss was on vacation, wiggling his toes in hot sand on a beach in the Caribbean. The year was 1976, and the boss was John Reed, the executive in charge of Citibank's checking account and credit card businesses. At every big New York bank, these lines of business were famous money losers; no one had been able to figure out how to make money on checking accounts and credit cards. (I know, hard to believe, right?) All the banks made a neat profit on business clients, but lost money on people like you and me. Reed was a rising star at Citibank; he'd just been put in charge and told to figure out a way to make these businesses profitable. He was facing a huge challenge. It was time to play.

I know, some of you might say, "Wait a minute, that guy makes a handsome salary, and his business is losing money — why does he deserve a vacation?" But Reed wasn't just being selfish; he knew that he often had his best ideas while playing. He carried a notepad and a pencil all over that Caribbean resort. And one day, lying in his beach chair staring out at the waves, he saw the solution. He reached for his pad and started writing . . .

That day on the beach, Reed wrote more than twenty pages. At the top of the first page, he put a title: "Memo from the Beach." Then he proceeded to draft the blueprint for a completely new kind of consumer bank. Customers could get their cash from a street-level machine; no need to wait in line for a teller. The machine could even tell you your account balance. Sounds familiar, right? But when Citibank installed ATMs all over Manhattan in 1980, it was the first and only bank in the world to have them.

"Memo from the Beach" also described a new way to market credit cards: nationally and through the mail. But in 1976 there were some old nineteenth-century banking laws still on the books that made this very difficult—banks couldn't market nationally because they had to deal with different lending laws in every state. When a Supreme Court ruling changed this in 1978, Citibank already had a strategy in place—right there in the "Memo from the Beach." All the company needed was to find a state willing to host its national credit card operations, and by 1980 Citibank had found a home. (Hint: It's not Delaware. See the bottom of the page for the answer.)

Today we take it for granted that we can get cash from a machine, twenty-four hours a day. We often take it for granted that our credit cards (and, alas, their monthly statements) come in the mail. But if Reed hadn't gone to the beach and made some space for his imagination to play, this might never have come to pass.

Exceptional creators are masters of the discipline of play, the ability to imagine and envision possible worlds.

envision possible worlds. Some of the most exceptional creators are also the most extreme players, as shown by researchers Robert and Michele Root-Bernstein. They interviewed ninety MacArthur Foundation genius grant recipients, and were surprised to find that quite a few of them engaged in what's called *worldplay*—the creation of elaborate imaginary worlds—when they were children.

Twenty-three of the ninety geniuses—about 25 percent—engaged in worldplay. (In a comparison group of typical undergraduate students, only twelve percent engaged in worldplay.) And most of those twenty-three geniuses felt sure there was a connection between their childhood worldplay and their creative success as adults.

Here's another intriguing discovery: guess how many of the extremely successful geniuses said that they engaged in worldplay as adults? A whopping 57 percent—that's

Worldplay (noun). The creation of an imagined world that organically builds over months, sometimes years. The world accumulates behind-the-scenes narratives, geographies, cultures, social and political institutions, and even ecosystems. The world is often documented in maps, in written stories, and with imaginary alphabets and languages.

Here are worldplay examples from two anonymous geniuses:

- The invented land of Mystica, inhabited by people and other creatures and replete with maps and histories
- A "rainbowhouse" in which the child "lived with imaginary animals and cartoons I loved" and bedtime stories woven around people who "lived in the clouds and at night would come into your dreams"

even more than said they had engaged in worldplay as children! One genius said: "In a real sense to do theory is to explore imaginary worlds because all models are simplified versions of reality, the world."

Another genius said:

My childhood was fairly rough and tumble, always racing around the neighborhood, building things, starting "businesses," coming up with new "inventions" (that never worked), launching ourselves into outer space, saving bugs in jars, digging holes to China—in memory, at least, all fresh, unfettered, and teeming with possibility. My work today is pretty much the same thing.

In the middle of one Saturday night in the fall of 1957, the whole thing . . . suddenly popped into my head, and I saw how to build a laser . . . But that flash of insight required the twenty years of work I had done in physics and optics to put all the "bricks" of the invention in there.

Gordon Gould, inventor of the laser

Play works because it taps into your subconscious mind—and research shows that great ideas usually emerge from the subconscious. They only arise after you've identified a good problem, in the first step (ask); and filled your mind, in the second and third steps (learn and look). Once you've fed your mind well, it's time for your subconscious to get to work, mixing all of those ideas together. The frustrating thing about this process is that you can't control it; the ideas come in unexpected zigs and zags, and they're not delivered on demand. You *can* clear the way for them, though, by using the practices and techniques in this chapter. Successful creators are highly sensitive to their subconscious mind, and they've developed a deep awareness of how (and when) to listen to it. By practicing the discipline of play, you nurture your mind's natural ability to create. You put your conscious mind into a state in which it's wide open, it's listening closely, it's waiting for these ideas to emerge. The techniques in this chapter are simply ways to get all the logic and criticism and rules and inhibitions out of the way.

The Practices

Play seems so instinctive—and it actually was, when you were five. But for creative adults, play can be enhanced by mastering four practices: Visualize, Relax, Find the Right Box, and Be a Beginner.

The First Practice of Playing: Visualize

Visualizing is really just imagining possible futures. The techniques of this practice teach you how to imagine freely, the way kids do when they create fantasy worlds with blocks or dolls—and the way MacArthur geniuses do when they create scientific theories, great works of art, or new business models.

> The early sources of the writer's craft can be linked to their playful explorations in childhood.
>
> *Vera John-Steiner, creativity researcher*

 Imagine Parallel Worlds

Pick one of the parallel worlds listed in the box. Now take whatever situation or problem you're puzzling over at the moment and try to envision it in that world's context. Or, try to think of ideas, images, or principles from that world that might be relevant to your problem.

Parallel Worlds

- Deer hunting
- Motorcycle customization
- Vegan cooking
- Prison
- Dentistry

- Lawn care
- Hairstyling
- Foreign affairs
- Air travel
- Furniture design
- The Catholic church
- Comics
- The Mafia
- The Olympics
- The circus
- Vacation resorts
- Alternative medicine

Make sure to pick a world that's familiar to you, but not at all related to the problem you're trying to solve.

One of my workshop students had been asked to create an oncology program that would be useful to Medicaid members. She chose furniture design as her alternate universe, and then she created this analogy: the frame of a sofa is like the bones of a body, and the fabric upholstery is like the skin, and the cushions are like the muscle tissue. For the sofa to be well designed, its structure has to be sound, its fabric has to look good, and its cushions have to be comfortable. That gave her three criteria by which to evaluate her program: structure, appearance and packaging, and user-friendly comfort and ease.

 Come Up with Fantastic Explanations

Stretch your imagination by using this technique whenever you find yourself relaxing outdoors, whether you're camping in the mountains or just stretched out in a hammock on a balmy summer afternoon. Clear away any practical worries or to-do checklists. Empty your brain. Absorb the air, gaze at the sky. Now think of a natural phenomenon that's a mystery to you, and come up with three wild and crazy stories to explain it. Your explanation should be obviously false, yet seem strangely plausible. I'll get you started with a first fantastic explanation for each:

- What causes disease?
    1. Evil spirits enter your body.
    2. _____
    3. _____
- Why is the sky blue?
    1. It's actually a big lake surrounding the earth.
    2. _____
    3. _____
- Why does it snow?
    1. Snow comes from a giant salt shaker, and an extraterrestrial monster is about to eat the entire planet.
    2. _____
    3. _____

It might help to imagine that you're a Stone Age human trying to figure out these natural phenomena without the benefit of modern science. Or that you're a three-year-old.

Envision What's Below

What's underneath you right now? Ceramic tile sprinkled with a few crumbs from the dog's Milk-Bone, okay. But what's underneath that? Keep drilling, right down to the center of the earth.

If you're outside of a city, you may live in a freestanding house, and below the floor might be just the earth. I live in a former coal-mining region where there's a good chance an abandoned mine is down there somewhere. I can envision some used Styrofoam coffee cups, empty chewing tobacco tins, some dirty bandanas that got left behind, maybe a few coins that dropped out of a miner's pocket.

If you're in a city, there will be many layers of stuff underneath you—especially if you're not on the ground floor of a building. Underground, there are likely to be tunnels for utilities, and possibly subway tunnels. Let your mind wander; the more details you can envision, the better.

 ### Follow the Long Arrow

Wherever you're sitting, envision a straight, invisible arrow shooting horizontally away from you. Imagine that it keeps going for at least a kilometer or a mile, parallel to the ground. Imagine moving out along that line, very slowly. As you go, identify all of the objects you pass through.

You're likely to be indoors while you're reading this, and if so, the first thing your arrow will hit is the wall. Move very slowly through the wallboard to the inside of the wall. Is there insulation? Wiring? In a minute you'll reach the wallboard on the other side of the wall and enter another room. Eventually you'll be outdoors. As your arrow continues, what's the next thing it hits?

Take your time—your arrow flies very slowly. Make sure to imagine everything it will pass through. At the end of a mile, envision exactly where your arrow is when it drops to the ground. What's around the arrow? Where is it resting, on what kind of ground? What do you hear and smell and see?

 ### Explore the Future

Travel five years into the future, and imagine that you've succeeded beyond your wildest dreams. What is your life like as a result? How has your success changed your circumstances? Write down as many details about this world as you can think of (using the present tense). Then write an imagined history of what's happened in the previous five years. Pretend you're working for a newspaper or a magazine and you're writing an article describing these events. Be sure to talk about the important decisions made five years ago (that is, today) that made the success possible.

Or imagine that you're being interviewed by a reporter who's writing a story about your success, and she's asking you the following questions (you might prefer to speak your answers into a voice recorder instead of writing them down):

Hint: It helps if you pick a specific magazine to be interviewed in that you respect and read regularly, like *Bloomberg Businessweek* if you're in business, or *ARTnews Magazine* if you're a painter.

- What's the best thing about achieving your goal?
- Why did you choose to pursue this goal?
- What was the first step you took to move toward it?
- Can you talk about one early obstacle, and how you got past it?
- Did anyone help you along the way?
- What advice would you give to someone with the same goal who is just starting out?

 Visualize Your Space

Close your eyes and imagine the place where you work. Spend some time looking around in your mind: visualize all of the furniture, what's hanging on the walls, the objects sitting on the desk. Imagine yourself walking around and touching the furniture, the walls, the objects. Identify a few things that irritate you. In my office, with piles of books on the floor, I'd probably imagine tripping over them!

Now, with your eyes still closed, adapt the image. Change anything you'd like to make it better. Money is no object. Rules don't exist.

The Second Practice of Playing: Relax

> Man's task is to become conscious of the contents that press upward
> from the unconscious.
>
> **Carl Jung**

The point of this practice is to step back and allow your mind to wander. These moments of distance and unfocusing are important; they give your mind some space, which it can then fill with new ideas.

The techniques in this practice help you develop enough trust and patience to let your subconscious work. You have to give it plenty of time to operate at its own pace, and then be alert when it's ready to deliver.

 Incubate

> He was busy absorbing his honey and filling the pigeonholes of his
> mind.
>
> **André Maurois**, French author, describing a period of several years
> when the French novelist Marcel Proust did not write a word

Creative people work harder than most other people— especially when they're engaged in the second step, learn. But, paradoxically, they also take more time off. That's because they know they have their best ideas when they're not working. People who work 365 days a year and never take a vacation rarely realize their creative potential. (Remember John Reed on the beach?)

Exceptional creators sleep more hours than the average person. Harvard researcher Jeffrey Ellenbogen found that after sleep, people are 33 percent more creative!

There's no creativity without some slack time. This is one of the most solid findings of creativity research.

Let incubation work its magic.

Relax.

Alas, this technique doesn't work very well if you're under a deadline; you can't force incubation. But trust in the creative process; ideas will come soon enough. The key is what you do *while* you're relaxing.

Unrelated, gently busy activities foster incubation because they keep you from thinking about your problem, puzzle, or challenge. Your mind has a chance to wander, and you get into a relaxed state in which your conscious mind pulls back a little.

Don't just snack and watch TV. Do something that engages your mind and body in a way that's totally different from your focused work time. Physical activity is particularly effective: your conscious mind focuses on the movement, freeing up the space your subconscious needs to sneak new ideas into awareness. Go out for coffee; take a walk; exercise; work in the garden; wash your car; repair an appliance.

Seymour Cray, the legendary designer of supercomputers, had an odd hobby: he spent countless hours digging an underground tunnel leading from the basement of his house in Chippewa Falls. Why? "I work for three hours and then get stumped," he explained. "So I quit and go to work in the tunnel. It takes me an hour or so to dig four inches and put in boards... Then I go up [to my lab] and work some more."

Unrelated, gently busy activities foster incubation because they keep you from thinking about your problem, puzzle, or challenge. Your mind has a chance to wander, and you get into a relaxed state in which your conscious mind pulls back a little, slackening the reins. Instead of tension, there's a little play, a little give.

The structural problems I set for myself in writing, in a long, snarled, frustrating and sometimes despairing morning of work, for instance, I can usually unsnarl by running in the afternoon.

Joyce Carol Oates

Most of these soothingly distracting activities aren't possible at work. So if you need a creative insight on the job, save a few mindless organizational tasks for such moments, or offer to clean out the break room fridge. Think of some way to create an incubation space at your office. (If your workplace culture says you have to "stay at your desk" and "always make sure you look busy," you're probably not in a creative environment. Maybe you can change it. If not, you might need to find sanctuary someplace else: at a nearby coffeehouse, or sitting on a bench on the landscaped grounds, or *in a new job* . . .).

Common Moments When Incubation Happens

- In the tub
- On the treadmill
- Gardening
- Mowing the lawn
- Sorting the recycling
- Waiting in the doctor's office
- Shopping
- Listening to talk show radio
- Listening to a boring lecture
- Sitting through a boring meeting
- Commuting to and from work

 Leave Something Undone

At the end of the day, don't try to finish the task completely. Leave a little bit unfinished. Then, the next morning, you'll find it easy to get started.

This technique is based on psychological studies that show that when you leave a task undone, "cognitive threads" are left dangling in your mind. (Remember the failure indices from the last chapter?) Before you start work again the next day, all of your nonwork activities—fixing and eating dinner, reading or watching television, getting ready for bed, sleeping, waking up, and showering—expose your mind to a broad variety of unrelated perceptions. If you're lucky, these unrelated perceptions will somehow hook on one of those hanging cognitive threads, and you'll have a sudden insight.

This is why there are so many stories of people having an inspiration during their morning shower, or when waking up in the middle of the night.

An old writer's trick is to retype the last page you wrote at the end of the previous day. You're typing what's familiar. Because it's easy, it lulls you into the writing mood, and you segue smoothly into the next sentence instead of staring at the old words for half an hour, waiting for inspiration.

Or try Ernest Hemingway's technique: he would never stop writing at the end of a chapter. Even if he happened to finish a chapter late at night, he would always continue for just a few more minutes, and would write the first paragraph of the next chapter. That way, the next day's start was much easier.

 ### *Still Your Mind*

Many people find that quiet time enhances their imagination and creativity. The key is to find a place where your mind can be quiet and your imagination can flourish.

Different people do this in different ways. For most people, this is a time for solitude. You might have a special chair, or a mat on the floor on which you can sit in the morning sun. Other people find that their imagination flourishes in

Now that cigarette smoking is banned in office buildings, many smokers use the outdoor cigarette break for this purpose. Nonsmokers should be granted the same opportunity to step outside regularly!

the social activity and the buzz of a local coffeehouse.

For effective meditation, seek out the right environment:

- It's away from the place where you do most of the conscious hard work.
- It's safe, familiar, and comfortable.
- There is no task or work visible.
- You are not rushed, and you're not going to be interrupted (no e-mail, no phone).

Some people find it easier to still their thoughts when their body is moving. The ancient practice of t'ai chi is described as "meditation in motion" because its slow, graceful gestures silence the mind so effectively. Sometimes a workbench in the garage, or an easel on the back porch, creates a place to meditate. Taking a long walk is a time-honored way to clear your head. Or consider getting a dog; the necessary daily walks are perfect, regular breaks for meditative thought.

 Listen

Even if you're reading this book in a fairly quiet place, there will be sounds around you—no place is completely quiet. Stop for a moment. Close your eyes. Breathe slowly and quietly. Listen to the everyday sounds you normally tune out:

- The clock ticking
- The fan of your computer or your home's furnace
- The sound of a truck driving by outside

The Third Practice of Playing: Find the Right Box

> Art consists of limitation. The most beautiful part of every picture is the frame.
>
> **G. K. Chesterton**

There's a popular belief that creativity comes from the absence of constraints. People assume that if you're not creative, it's because you're thinking inside the box—so all you need to do is get rid of the box!

But research shows just the opposite: creativity is enhanced by constraints. They just have to be the *right* constraints. The techniques of this section show you how important it is to draw boundaries around the space in which you play. If you're stumped for an idea, maybe you just need to play with different toys for a while; start a new game, with a different set of rules.

 ### *Be Specific*

List as many white things as you can. Try to think of objects like chalk that are white by definition, not objects like cars or shirts that are only occasionally white.

Now, list as many white, edible things as you can.

_____

_____

_____

_____

_____

_____

_____

_____

_____

_____

_____

The surprise for most people is that this second list is usually as long as the first! Why didn't you think of all of those items in the first part of the exercise? It's because *more specific instructions result in greater creativity* than do vague, open-ended instructions.

Beginning improv actors are taught to be specific when they propose new dramatic ideas. Instead of saying, "Look, it's a gun!" it's better to say, "Oh my god, it's the X-300 destroyer ray gun!" The second version makes it easier for your partner on stage to come up with a more creative reply. That seems counterintuitive, because the first version leaves your partner with a lot more options. But it works every time.

Draw the Right Box

> When great designers think outside the box, what they're really doing
> is wearing the glasses of totally different disciplines.
>
> **Tom Kelley, CEO of the design firm IDEO**

Connect the four dots shown here by drawing two connected, straight lines without lifting your pencil from the paper between the first and second line. (Hint: You can't do it unless you draw outside of the trapezoid that's formed by connecting the dots.)

●　●

●　　　●

Turn to the next page for the solution.

The solution is an inverted V, with the lines extending above the top dots.

Now, see if you can connect these dots by drawing four connected straight lines, without lifting your pencil from the paper. (Hint: In this one, just like before, you'll have to go outside the dots.)

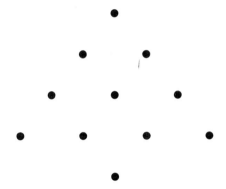

If you haven't gotten it yet, the next page helps you out by giving you the first line. Stay with me here; there's a reason to continue doing each exercise.

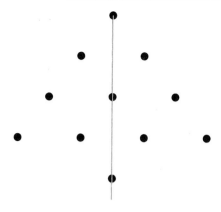

Give yourself a minute to think about it before turning to the next page for the answer.

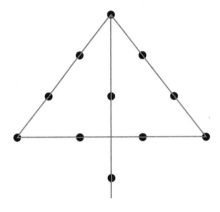

Now, connect the four dots that follow by adding two more lines, starting at either end of the first line that's already drawn.

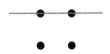

(Hint: Both lines have to go outside the box to make this work. If you're still stumped, the answer is at the bottom of this page.)

The two lines form a V that extends down beneath the bottom two dots.

Now, that was all just practice. Here's a problem that should give you a bit more of a challenge. Connect these nine dots by drawing four connected lines without lifting your pencil:

•   •   •

•   •   •

•   •   •

Of course, you could use the three-line zig zag solution on the cover of this book, if you imagine the dots as marbles, or if you draw a very thick line—with a fat crayon, for example. And that's definitely a creative solution! But with small dots and a normal pencil, you'll need four lines.

If you haven't gotten it after a minute, look at the hint at the bottom of this page. (The solution is at the end of this chapter.)

Without the proper training, the nine-dot problem is extremely hard; hardly anyone can solve it. The nine-dot problem is usually called an "insight" problem, because it's supposed to require a flash of creative insight to figure out that "you have to go outside the box." In fact, the cliché *started* with this classic puzzle.

You have to go outside the box two times.

But the solution is *not* about thinking outside the box; it's about finding the right box. Now that you've solved similar problems, it's a lot easier. You don't need a blinding flash of insight, because you already know how to solve "outside the dots" problems.

After all that practice, you're now a pro. Are you ready for the sixteen-dot problem?

Without lifting your pencil, draw six straight lines that connect all sixteen dots. (Hint: Every line must go outside the box. The solution is at the end of this chapter.)

 Create a New Box

Invent your own tiny area, or box, of expertise, one that takes you only an hour or two to master. Some examples:

- Buy a motorcycle magazine and tear out all of the advertisements for protective clothing. Look through them closely and watch for the common features. Now you're an expert in "how to lay out motorcycle magazine ads."

- Photograph the same scene with every possible setting on your camera. Now you've attained an expertise most camera owners never acquire: you understand how different settings change the image.

- Watch every YouTube video on how to tie a bow tie or a scarf. Now you can teach your kids.

- Go out in the yard. Pull up twenty blades of grass and take them inside. Carefully split each blade of grass in half, lengthwise. In ten minutes, you're an expert in "how to split blades of grass."

- The next time you're in a diner, or any restaurant that has those napkin dispensers on the table, open up the dispenser and take out all of the napkins. Figure out how the spring works to make sure the napkins always stay right at the opening. In five minutes, you're an expert in napkin dispenser mechanics.

Successful creators are playful and inquisitive. When you live your life with a playful attitude, you develop an instinct to spend five minutes here and there mastering tiny boxes—just like children at play learn everything about how marbles roll on different carpet textures, or how a Slinky travels down the stairs. Before you know it, you're an expert in hundreds of tiny boxes. And that's when good things start to happen unexpectedly—because good ideas come from blending lots of different tiny boxes.

> Prepare a list of five boxes—perhaps the parallel worlds at the beginning of this chapter—and analyze and explain your creative challenge in each of them, one by one.

 Use Every Box

Which of the following letters is different?

A   E   I   F   U

Most people will say *F* because it's the only consonant. But every one of these five letters is different in a different way. Look at each letter in turn, and find something that makes it different from the others.

The Fourth Practice of Playing:
Be a Beginner

> In the beginner's mind there are many possibilities; in the expert's mind there are few.
>
> **Shunryu Suzuki, Zen monk**

Zen Buddhists have beginner's minds; gamblers have beginner's luck. And anyone trying to be creative needs to begin all over again every day so ideas will be fresh.

We start over again reluctantly; beginning is hard. It's so much easier to just recycle a solution that worked the last time. But beginning is exciting, too; everything is new, and all things are possible.

The techniques of this practice nudge you into the childlike state of not knowing. As you try each technique, notice how that beginner's mind-set feels, and try to take its wide-open innocence back to your own area of expertise. Become a beginner again and again.

 Do Something for the First Time

When was the last time you did something for the first time?

Try ...

- Hula-Hooping
- Juggling
- Playing harmonica
- Baking bread
- Building a card tower

 Start a New Hobby

Experiment with a new hobby. It can be something classic:

- Model trains
- Wood carving
- Basket weaving

Or you could try something new, such as

- Starting a blog
- Building a Web site
- Uploading a video to YouTube
- Making a video by editing footage from your last family holiday

 Plan on Fun

Keep a written list of fun activities that you'd like to do someday. You could ...

- Take cooking classes
- Go skydiving
- Race a motorcycle
- Sign up for a writing workshop
- Take piano lessons
- Learn archery

Add to the list as you hear about new opportunities and develop new interests. Resolve to do something from the list at least once each year.

Onward ...

We've gotten through the first four steps, and I haven't said anything about how to have creative ideas! And yet these first four steps are the secret to a successful, creative life. When you engage in these four steps, your mind becomes a creative engine, generating ideas nonstop.

So now we're ready for the fifth step, think, generating creative ideas. You can't jump ahead to the fifth step; you won't have

The creative mind plays with the objects it loves.

Carl Jung

truly creative ideas without first going through these four steps. But now that you've made it to this point, you're ready for techniques to increase your brain's productivity.

Solutions

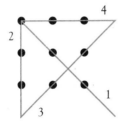

Nine-dot problem.

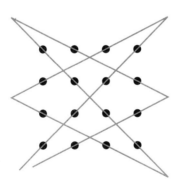

Sixteen-dot problem.

THE FIFTH STEP
THINK

**How to Have Way More Ideas
Than You'll Ever Need**

The best way to get a good idea is to have a lot of ideas.
Linus Pauling, two-time Nobel laureate

Here's a snapshot of how some of history's most famous creators managed to create their masterpieces:

- Pablo Picasso produced about twenty thousand pieces of art.
- Albert Einstein wrote more than 240 scientific papers.
- Johann Sebastian Bach composed a cantata every week.
- Thomas Edison filed over one thousand patents.
- Richard Branson started 250 companies.
- Joyce Carol Oates published forty-five novels, thirty-nine story collections, eight poetry collections, five dramas, and nine essay collections.

Sounds impressive, right? But the majority of Edison's patents never made him a dime. Most of Einstein's scientific papers go uncited by other scientists. Most of Picasso's artworks are not hanging on the walls at the world's top art museums.

And it doesn't matter. These people are famous because a special few of their creations were genius.

Sheer productivity is the way of virtually all great creators. Poet Stephen Spender explained, "My method is to write down as many ideas as possible, in however rough a form in notebooks. I have at least 20 of these going back 15 years." One of his notebooks had over one hundred pages of writing. Later he went back through those pages, and each time he noticed a good new idea, he made a special mark in the margin. From a hundred pages of ideas, only six poems eventually emerged.

Six very good poems.

Composer Aaron Copland once remarked:

> Most composers keep a notebook in which they put down germinal ideas that occur to them, thinking "well, we'll work on that later." You can't pick the moment when you are going to have ideas. It picks you and then you might be completely absorbed in another piece of work. You put the ideas down where you can find them later, when you need to look for ideas and they don't come easily.

The creative life is filled with lots of small ideas. The small ideas weave together as you travel along the zig zag path, and they can lead you to greatness.

Professor Dean Keith Simonton, a psychologist on the faculty of UC Davis, became fascinated by these stories of high productivity. After all, sheer volume isn't really what you'd expect to result in great creativity. You'd think the best, most creative works would be the ones the creator worked on for years, carefully crafting and fine-tuning. And with all of that time invested in a single work, the most creative people should actually generate less work overall, right?

Simonton decided to see if this pattern always held by mathematically exploring the relationship between quantity of output and exceptional creativity. In one massive study, he created a database with information about hundreds of the world's most creative scientists. The database contains an entry for every scientific paper published by these scientists, and it records which year each paper was published and how old the scientist was at the time. Simonton then counted up the number of times other scientists cited a paper in their own work, as a measure of the creative impact of the original paper.

He discovered that the famous stories of high productivity aren't unusual. For all creators in all fields, the most creative works are generated by the most productive scholars. Simonton's four key discoveries have big implications for how we can enhance our everyday creativity.

> **The research is clear: the best way to come up with creative ideas is to come up with a *lot* of ideas.**

First, he found that the great majority of papers are never cited. Remember, we're talking about the world's most successful scientists here! And yet most of their works had no visible impact on other scholars. And the few works that did gain a foothold were only cited once or twice. Only a tiny percentage of papers received more than one hundred citations, and among these were the supercreative works of genius that changed the world.

When I read Simonton's findings, I wondered if maybe the pattern he found only held for scientists who were less creative. Maybe the brilliant ones—the ones with the Nobel Prizes—were more consistently successful? No, it turns out; the second key discovery is that even the most famous scientists have published quite a few papers that are never cited. The best example is Einstein: he wrote 240, and only a handful made a major impact. (Paradoxically, the most creative scientists actually publish more *unimportant* papers than mediocre scientists, simply because they're publishing so much!)

Third, the scientists who published the most papers in their career were the ones who were judged to be the most creative by their peers. Lifetime quantity turns out to be a pretty good predictor of creative quality—*and* reputation.

Fourth, when you look year by year at a scientist's career, in the year when one of his or her top papers was published, that scientist published more papers overall than in other years. You can usually predict when a scientist's best paper was published simply by looking at the total volume of creative output in that year.

Simonton conducted this study for contemporary scientists and for nineteenth-century scientists, and he found that the pattern held across the generations. He's done the same study with composers and other fine artists, and he found the same pattern in their work, too.

The research is clear: the best way to come up with creative ideas is to come up with a *lot* of ideas.

But how?

The Practices

The three practices in this chapter—Ideate, Transform, and Schedule—show you how to turn yourself into an idea machine.

The First Practice of Thinking: Ideate

> Nothing is more dangerous than having just one idea.
>
> *Émile-Auguste Chartier, French philosopher and writer*

Dean Keith Simonton's research shows that the key to successful creativity is quantity. The most exceptional creators are known for their sheer volume of ideas. But if you're used to pondering for hours and finally coming up with a single, precious idea that you're scared to tweak for fear you'll lose it . . . how do you loosen up and start more ideas flowing?

Think Different

Each day, select a common household object. Pick one from this list, or just look around the room:

- Paper clip
- Coat hanger
- Broom
- Comb
- Brick
- Refrigerator magnet
- Pencil
- Knife

Once you've selected an object, get a piece of paper and give yourself five minutes to list as many unusual uses as you can for this item. For example, a brick can be a doorstop, a paperweight, a weapon . . . Or it can be a pedestal, a mud scraper, a hammer, a window prop, a meat pounder, a platform, a drain cover . . . Come up with ideas as quickly as you can; don't stop to think about whether they're any good, or whether they're unusual enough. Don't edit yourself at all. The key is to come up with a long list of ideas.

This technique exercises the part of your brain that's responsible for *divergent thinking*—the term psychologists use when you generate multiple possibilities. Divergent thinking got its name because your mind "diverges" to explore a broad range of possibilities. It's the opposite of what most tests measure, *convergent thinking*—which occurs when you're asked to "converge" on the single, right answer. Creative people are particularly good at divergent thinking.

Look back at your list of unusual uses. One measure of creativity is the length of your list; your ability to generate a long list is what psychologists call *fluency*. But that's not necessarily the best measure of creativity, because your ideas might be very common. In fact, when researchers ask people to generate unusual uses in the laboratory, the same ideas keep coming up. (When I started to think about a brick, I thought doorstop and paperweight—not terribly original.) So a second measure of creativity is how many *rare* ideas you think of. Psychologists call this *originality*, and it's an important component of divergent thinking. It turns out that people who generate the longest lists wind up having the most original ideas—and this is why quantity of ideas results in greater creativity. You push past the obvious.

Another possibility is that all the ideas on your list are pretty similar to each other. If all of your brick ideas are types of weapons—a projectile, a bomb, a knife—that's less creative than if you come up with a broader variety of ideas. So psychologists also use this "unusual uses" technique to evaluate *flexibility*—defined as how many different idea categories your ideas span.

All three aspects of divergent thinking—fluency, originality, and flexibility—are important to creativity. But in one experiment after another, researchers have found that all three are highly correlated, meaning that the surest way to greater creativity is simply to come up with the most ideas possible. The longer your list, the likelier it is that some of your ideas will be original, and that you'll break out of the safe confines of a single category.

Here's another technique that will increase your divergent thinking ability. Roll a six-sided die, and use the number that comes up to select one of the following questions:

1. How would the world be different if you had two thumbs on each hand?

2. How would the world be different if no one died—everyone lived forever?

3. How would the world be different if there were five sexes?

4. How would the world be different if gravity stopped for one second each day?

5. How would the world be different if people no longer needed or wanted sleep?

6. How would the world be different if both men and women could have babies?

Imagine how that world would be different from ours. Get a piece of paper, and list as many specific facts about this alternate universe as you can. The most important thing is the length of your list—force yourself to keep going, and generate as long a list as you can. Don't slow down by thinking too hard about whether any one fact is a good idea or not—just keep writing ideas. Your list should have at least ten items, but if you're good at imagining, you might come up with many more.

As with the unusual uses technique, this technique exercises your brain's ability to generate lots of ideas. The value of these techniques is that they get you into the habit of generating ideas, and they also help you practice keeping going even when you feel stumped. We're all conditioned, in school and work, to think critically about every idea that occurs to us. But if we're critical too soon (see Chapter Seven), we silence the creative parts of our brain. So, avoid thinking critically, and don't stop. What usually happens is, just as soon as you're sure you've run out of good ideas and you're only writing lousy ones . . . a really good idea will pop into your head.

 Try Toppling

Toppling is a form of free association—the classic psychoanalytic technique where you're asked to say the first word that comes into your head. Therapists use free association because they think it will tap into your unconscious mind. With toppling, you take advantage of the power of free association to tap into the unconscious, but with a twist that helps you learn how to manage your unconscious to greater creative advantage.

Pick a random word and do a free association, just like you're on the therapist's couch. Or start with one of the words in the word list provided as part of this technique: pick any one of the words, then think of another word inspired by that word. Keep going—free-associate a third word from the second word—but add a twist: every new word has to be associated with the last one in a new way, so they have a different kind of connection than the previous pair had. For example, if you start with "mushroom," don't do "mushroom," "carrot," "potato"; that just gets you a long list of vegetables. It's fine that your second word is "carrot," but now look for an association from "carrot" that has nothing to do with food. Why not "stick," as in carrot and stick? If you keep going this way, you might come up with a list like this:

1. Mushroom.
2. Carrot (both are vegetables).
3. Stick (as in carrot and stick). You could also say "sight" (eating carrots is good for your eyes); or "ground" (carrots are root vegetables and grow in the ground); or "top" to describe a redhead.
4. Glue (as in glue stick). You could also say "eyes" (you can put your eye out while playing with a stick); "up" (as in a stickup); "needle"; or even "gymnastics" (when you "stick" a landing, you land standing straight up).
5. Scissors (both glue and scissors are often found in your desk drawer).
6. Rock (as in the game "Rock-Paper-Scissors").
7. Scotch (as in drinking scotch whisky on the rocks).

To generate the word list that follows I spent a day thumbing through the dictionary, looking for words filled with action, words with multiple meanings, and words that lend themselves to connections.

Word List

Pocket	Breeze	Smell
Worm	Cymbal	Galaxy
Theater	Cloud	Bedroom
Tightrope	Monster	Vapor
Lobster	Ladybug	Picture
Pearl	Militia	Hurricane
Blink	Gift	Fart
Motorcycle	Weed	Gallery
Shadow	Palace	Umbrella
Keyboard	Piñata	Filter
Ferment	Scarf	Wildfire
Window	Flash	Pick
Clutch	Hatch	Climax
Wine	Obsolete	Island
Stick	Continue	Seed
Litter	Desert	Noose
Overdose	Pavement	Skyscraper
Parade	Drizzle	Mirror
Recovery	Float	Gentleman
Tourist	Prison	Campfire
Election	Radiate	Helicopter
Frosting	Feather	Curve
Smell	Publicity	Sucker
Shrink	Bullet	Horror
Divorce	Evergreen	Reflex
Trash	Settlement	Projectile
Trick	Lattice	Jet
Mushroom	Pipeline	Trash
Cartoon	Country	Popcorn
Wrapping paper	Apology	Wedge
Outlaw	Disciple	Clone

Workout	Catalog	Crush
Eyeball	Fiber	Rainy day
Scatter	Jelly bean	Balance
Fashion	Cactus	Center
Farm	Machine gun	Back
Rake	Taste buds	Crown
Reservation	Dashboard	Room service
Posture	Library	Pirate
Network	Onion rings	Clamp
Naked	Stamp	Wind
Battery	Criminal	Scaffold
Juggle	Roach	Harmony
Comfort	Lecture	Rabbit
Playground	Double	Mask
Elevator	Marble	Reunion
Guard	Bottle	Screw
Tiptoe	Visitor	Pervert
Paisley	Winter	Dump
Hammer	Laminate	Homecoming
Engineer	Silhouette	Deodorant
Atom	Board	Gondola
Meltdown	Minister	Bookend
Organ	Dwarf	Drop
Song	Orgy	Sideline
Shoeshine	Speech	Perfect
Newspaper	Rent	Magic
Plastic	Kiss	Equation
Scissors	Instant	Sponge
Fiddle	Index card	Inflate
Vacation	Pilgrimage	Quarter
Grade	Deal	Factory
Greenhouse	Torture	Barrel

Monument	Gunpowder	Underwear
Exile	Stage	Crystal
Fraction	Entry	Nucleus
Luggage	Joint	Roller skate
Emergency	Bag	Introduction
Slit	Oracle	Garden
Reaction	Collect	Turtle
Nausea	Ponytail	Twist
Foreplay	Flag	Vacation
Machete	Pastry	Shatter
Freeze	Sandstorm	Stranger
Riddle	Motto	Hardware
Hurdle	Muscle	Impostor
Compass	Starve	Misfire
Guess	Abacus	Fire escape
Level	Mailbox	Haircut
Battle	Panic	Channel
Casket	Pollinate	Huddle
Diameter	Idiot	Improvise
Receipt	Pollen	Surgery
Saddle	Parallel	Stroke
Spring	Football	Microscope
Intercept	Sneak	Aspirin
Complement	Fold	Vibrate
Hangover	Dictator	Skull
Absorb	Gladiator	Brush
Pinpoint	Houseboat	Bang
Maze	Wash	Operation
Accordion	Periscope	Button
Parrot	Rainbow	Normal
Church	Proof	

Toppling exercises your mind's ability to generate ideas by association, joining two separate words by recognizing a relationship between them. Psychologists have discovered that all ideas are combinations of existing concepts, and that the best new ideas result from combining concepts that are more different from each other. Toppling forces you to keep coming up with new, more distant associations.

Toppling also increases your flexibility—your mental ability to generate ideas in a broad range of categories.

The word list provided here is just a start; you can choose your own way to identify a starting word. Just make sure it's random. Open a book to any page and pick the first word of the fifth line on the page. Or eavesdrop on a conversation and use the first noun you hear.

After practicing toppling a couple of times, try to apply the technique to a creative challenge you're facing right now. This time, instead of generating a list of words, generate a sentence at each step. Don't force it too quickly, but try to eventually reach an idea that's related to your problem. Let's say my problem is that when it rains, my window leaks, and caulking around the window's edge doesn't seem to fix it.

If the word is "rake":

1. Rake.
2. I'm raking up the leaves.
3. The leaves of my table are stored in the basement.
4. Spiders always seem to build webs in my basement.
5. Spiders get into the house through small cracks.
6. Rain gets into the house through small cracks—there must be a crack in the window frame itself!

You might not get there after the second or the third sentence, but keep going until you get a sentence related to your problem. The power of this technique is that it leads your mind toward your creative challenge in a non-linear, unpredictable way, and its circuitous associations are more likely to lead you to an answer that hasn't already occurred to you.

The best new ideas result from combining concepts that are more different from each other.

Toppling Towelettes

Steven Paley's company Texwipe sold foil-enclosed towelettes that were used in the electronics industry to remove oils from circuit boards and other equipment. The towelettes were soaked with 91 percent isopropyl alcohol. One day the company got a letter from a police officer in Florida. He had somehow gotten one of these foil-enclosed towelettes and wanted to know where to buy more. He explained why: "Every day I deal with criminals and the scum of the earth... When I come home to my family at night, I need to disinfect myself from my work."

The word "disinfect" jumped out at Paley, and it gave him an idea for a new market: he could sell disinfecting towelettes to the general consumer. Now millions of these foil packets are sold, and you can find them everywhere. Paley didn't need to come up with a new invention; he just needed a new context.

The Second Practice of Thinking: Transform

The first practice, Ideate, is the best way to start enhancing your ability to think. Once you've mastered those techniques, though, you're ready for the second practice: Transform. Its three techniques build on the first practice, showing you how to take the ideas you generate and transform them in surprising ways.

SCAMPER

SCAMPER is an acronym: each of the seven letters stands for a specific method for coming up with new ideas by transforming existing ideas. The seven methods corresponding to the seven letters are

- Substitute
- Combine
- Adapt
- Magnify or Modify
- Put to other uses
- Eliminate
- Rearrange or Reverse

> Ideas are like rabbits. You get a couple and learn how to handle them and pretty soon you have a dozen.
>
> *John Steinbeck*

These methods are especially useful if you're creating with physical materials—inventing a new machine, maybe, or solving a problem with your car or house. You can still use SCAMPER with abstract, conceptual creativity, like the kind associated with science or poetry, but it's a bit harder.

Here's an example: I like to drink my Diet Coke with ice, but the ice always melts too fast, and my soda gets watery before I finish. How can I keep my soda cold without diluting it?

Let's try each of the seven methods. The key is to force yourself to come up with something for each of the seven, even though some of them will be quite a challenge.

- *Substitute.* Replace the ice with something else. Maybe instead of using water, I could put the soda itself in the freezer. The first time I try this, I explode a can of Diet Coke all over our frozen vegetables. The second time, I make sure to take it out while it's still slushy, not frozen solid.

- *Combine.* Combine the soda with ice. I make ice cubes by using soda. I fill an ice cube tray with Diet Coke. Much less hazardous.

- *Adapt.* Adapt the ice cubes so they don't melt. Perhaps the cubes could be plastic shapes filled with water, so the water would freeze but also stay inside the cube while it is chilling my drink?

- *Magnify or Modify.* Make each ice cube bigger; then there'll be a lower ratio of surface area to volume, and it'll melt more slowly.

- *Put to other uses.* Put the soda to other uses besides drinking. That doesn't make sense. But what if I put the *glass* to another use? I could make a glass of a material that itself freezes, so that the glass chills the drink.

- *Eliminate.* Eliminate the ice from the drink—then there will be no melting and no dilution. But now the problem is, the drink doesn't get cold. But I could chill the drink itself (see Substitute).

- *Rearrange or Reverse.* How about if I rearrange the ice, soda, and glass, so that the ice is on the *outside* of the glass? (OK, this is similar to "Put to other uses," but I'm counting it!)

After I made this list I went searching on the Internet and discovered that many of these ideas are already products. You can buy a glass that you put in the freezer, so that the glass chills your drink. You can buy reusable plastic ice cubes that chill your drink without melting into it. But my favorite solution was to fill a special ice cube tray with Diet Coke, so when the cubes melt and cool the drink there's no dilution at all. I now do this daily. The only problem is when my son forgets and cools his Kool-Aid with Diet Coke!

SCAMPER Yourself

One of my workshop participants tried SCAMPER's Magnify method to figure out how to advance in his company. He was working in a pigeonholed position, in an organization that was highly siloed. So his idea was to *magnify* the need to collaborate and communicate by creating small creativity groups that would bring workers from different departments together. Once the need was magnified and then met, the practice would create a "new normal," and small, simple acts of collaboration would feel more natural. His pigeonhole would have breathing space, and he could begin to network in a way that wouldn't have been possible before the small-group initiative.

Another participant used Rearrange or Reverse to break an impasse with workers at his company. They had a "zero-incident" goal, meaning zero injuries, and workers seemed pretty indifferent to the prescribed safety practices. How could he get past the machismo and persuade them to take the goal seriously? He flipped the logic and asked the workers to argue for *unsafe* behavior—Why was it better? He asked the safety representatives to argue that more recorded incidents per month would be better for business. He made his point.

 List Attributes

Listing attributes works equally well for physical challenges and for abstract, conceptual challenges. This technique is so powerful, it can help you come up with all possible creative solutions to a problem.

For example, I often wonder—as I sit in traffic—"How can I reduce the length of my commute to work?"

Start by deconstructing the problem, breaking it into its component parts. For my commute problem, I decided its components were

- Reduce
- Length
- Commute
- Work

The second step is to examine each of those components and list its attributes. For example, the attributes of *work* are:

1. Work is what I do to make money.
2. Work is at the office.
3. Work is Monday through Friday.
4. At work, I have a boss.
5. At work, I have a project with a schedule and a deadline.

Once you get a list of attributes for each component, coming up with ideas becomes a lot easier. Focus on each attribute and try to modify or improve it, generating new ideas using the SCAMPER verbs. Here's part of what I came up with for my commute problem:

1. Work is what I do to make money. (*Reverse*: I don't need money. Or, I make money some other way. Maybe I could start my own business and work from home?)
2. Work is at the office. (*Magnify*: Work is everywhere. Maybe I could work from home?)
3. Work is Monday through Friday. (*Reverse*: Work is on the weekend. If I can go to work on the weekend, the commute will be shorter because fewer people will be doing it.)

These aren't such bad ideas! Now let's try the attributes of *commute*:

1. Commuting is how I get to work. (*Reverse*: Commuting brings work to me. Maybe I could telecommute using the Internet?)

2. I commute in a car. (*Substitute*: Maybe public transportation would get me to work faster? Or maybe I could carpool and get some work done on the way, on those days when I'm not driving?)

3. There's always a lot of traffic. (*Eliminate*: Drive to work at an unusual time, when there's less traffic.)

This technique can take a lot of time, coming up with all of the attributes for all of the components, but the upside is that it generates a huge list of potential creative solutions.

Reverse Again

After hearing dozens of painful stories of divorce and the hardship it caused for young children, I heard a story about a divorcing couple that I've never forgotten. After many long conversations about who would keep the house, who the children would live with, and where, these parents came up with a solution that reversed the usual logic: *they decided to let the kids keep the house.* The dad moved across the street, the mom to an apartment close by, and they took turns moving back to the family home to take care of the kids. The kids didn't have to get shuttled around; they stayed put. The solution was more logical, kinder to the blameless children, and far less disruptive to their world.

Whoever said that in a divorce one parent should have to leave and the other should get to stay? Whoever said the kids should be the ones who have to move in and out? Often when you're stumped and having trouble coming up with good ideas, it's because you're making assumptions about your problem that turn out not to be true. Creativity researchers call these "unwarranted assumptions," and creative insights tend to pop right out once you recognize and remove them.

The real problem is, it's hard to know what you're assuming, because the assumption is often made unconsciously. You don't know which assumptions are absolute and which ones are unwarranted. This technique helps you figure that out.

Start by listing all of the assumptions you've made. Be very detailed and elaborate. Let's say my problem is not having enough money to pay my bills every month. Here are some assumptions I'm making:

1. My salary stays the same every month.
2. My bills stay the same every month.
3. If I don't pay my bills, bad things will happen—the electricity will get turned off, the doctor will stop seeing me, and my credit rating will be horrible.

Now look at each assumption one by one, and write down its opposite.

1. My salary increases every month.
2. My bills decline every month.
3. If I don't pay my bills, nothing bad will happen.

Usually when you do this, the reverse sounds pretty crazy. But that's important; that craziness is what has the potential to spark some surprising new ideas in the third step. That's when you ask yourself, "What sequence of events might lead to a situation in which this reversal is true?" Maybe you find a way to take on freelance work that's more and more successful. Maybe you get creative about trimming your expenses. Maybe you skip town!

Reverse the Assumptions

Joe Adams, a legendary private detective and former mercenary, was once brought into a Chesterfield, Missouri, kidnapping case by a stumped police department. A teenage girl had been missing for six months—no ransom note, no clues. Adams didn't beat around the bush: he said he didn't want to take a case that couldn't be resolved. The police officer took a deep breath, then admitted, "We think she's dead."

After talking to her parents, Adams decided to take the case, but he refused to think about it as a body-recovery situation. Instead, he flipped the assignment and made it his goal to "find the perp," not the girl. He figured that once he found the kidnapper, he'd also find the girl, one way or another. He followed the trail all the way to Costa Rica, even though customs records showed that the girl had not left the United States. Sure enough, he found the kidnapper—and befriended him—and learned that he'd stashed the girl with a friend in a Mennonite community in Iowa until she came of age and he could marry her. She was recovered alive and well by a SWAT team.

You can do Reverse Again in combination with List Attributes. After you've got your list of attributes, try reversing each of them. Take my commute problem again:

1. What if I didn't need money? What if there were another way to get it? (Working at home?)

2. What if I could work somewhere else? (Working at a different place closer to home?)

3. What if there were no schedule? (I could then commute to work during times with less traffic.)

The Third Practice of Thinking: Schedule

> Beware the barrenness of a busy life.
>
> **Socrates**

In his psychology research, Mihaly Csikszentmihalyi has found that exceptional creators, from all walks of life, schedule in daily idea time. No matter how busy they are, they guard their idea time religiously. The reason's simple: you'll have more ideas if you devote more time to having ideas. The techniques of this third practice can help you stick with a schedule that builds in time for creativity.

 Set an Idea Time

Playwright and poet Julia Cameron, author of *The Artist's Way*, started taking time every day to write "morning pages"—three pages of writing about anything. "As I wrote those pages," she noted, "new ideas began to walk in." In *The Artist's Way*, she suggests that you take thirty minutes every morning to freewrite in a journal.

Maybe you think better at midnight, though. Develop a creativity schedule, regularly blocking out a time when your mind will be both sharp and relaxed, unhurried and undistracted. Start by looking inward to learn what time of day works best for you for generating new ideas, gathering fresh information, and reflecting critically. For many people, it's first thing in the morning; others prefer a break right after lunch, or take time late at night when the pressures of the day have subsided.

Many of the world's most innovative companies have made this technique standard practice. For example, at W. L. Gore—a company responsible for breakthrough innovations like Gore-Tex waterproof fabric and Glide dental floss—employees are told to spend 10 percent of each week thinking up new ideas. At Google, it's 20 percent. At 3M—where the business practice first originated—it's 15 percent.

Set an Idea Quota

Give yourself a daily idea quota. Make it simple: "I promise to come up with ten ideas every day." If you have trouble producing new ideas every day, then try this:

On Monday morning, pose a specific problem. Then commit to generating six solutions every day for the entire week. For example, last week I chose this problem: "How can I make my daily commute more productive?" On Monday, my six ideas were

1. Making important calls on my cell phone.

2. Inventing a new device that projects a computer screen onto the windshield—and understands spoken commands.

3. Taking public transportation instead of driving so I can do work on the way.

4. Working at home some of the time to reduce the commute time.

5. Moving closer to work.

6. Using my commute time to come up with my six ideas a day!

On Tuesday, it will be harder, because on Monday most people come up with the obvious ideas. But force yourself to keep at it. (Listening to audiobooks, memorizing poetry, using a voice memo recorder . . .) By Wednesday, some of your ideas will get pretty silly (singing my to-do list). But crazy, ridiculous ideas are okay too! By Thursday or Friday, you might be getting frustrated because most of your ideas will be downright wacky (isometric exercises, anyone?). But keep going, because this is when you're most likely to generate a surprisingly good idea (Oxford lectures on my iPod!).

Lowry Burgess, a professor of art at Carnegie Mellon, gave his art students an assignment: make 200 two-by-four-foot drawings in two weeks. On the first day, one of his students, the business author Jeff Mauzy, gathered a few interesting objects, put them together on a table, and took a few hours to draw a still life. Then he rearranged the objects and drew another still life. By the end of the first day he'd done only five drawings—that was far too slow a pace to get 200 finished in fourteen days. So he started moving faster. He sketched outlines, doodled quick impressions, churned out multiple variations on a single still life. After 90 drawings, each new one had started to look like a child's scribble. After 60 more of these—he was now up to 150 drawings—Mauzy became bored with the rapid scribbling and decided to try something new. He laid six sheets of paper on his driveway, revved his motorcycle, and drove over the paper. The result was less than inspiring: faint images of tire tracks crossed the sheets. Although they didn't look great, they inspired Mauzy to try something similar: he put six sheets in a row in his front yard, and then he climbed onto the roof of his house and dribbled paint on the sheets from above. Now he was on a roll. He thought of one idea after another, all different ways of creating a series of six drawings together. Back inside, he taped one sheet to a wall, crumpled five others into balls, and pasted them to the first sheet. He kept going.

Burgess's assignment wasn't unusual; students at art schools all over the United States have been given the same challenge. The reason this outrageous assignment is so effective is that it trains students in the discipline of thinking. And when you're forced to keep generating ideas to reach a quota, you typically go through the same process that Mauzy did:

1. At first, the ideas are predictable and ordinary.
2. Then, you enter a phase of fatigue, where the ideas are uninspired.
3. Finally, you start to surprise yourself with unexpected new ideas.

Onward . . .

Most people associate creativity with new ideas. But the fifth step, think, is only one of the eight steps required for successful creativity. If you skip the first four steps, no amount of creativity training can help you come up with creative ideas.

If you've mastered the first four steps, however, the techniques in this chapter will predictably and reliably help you generate surprising new ideas.

That's not the end of the process, though. Ideas are cheap. To be successfully creative, you need to take your ideas forward to the final three steps. The next, sixth step, fuse, will teach you how to combine ideas, bringing them together for more powerful and effective creativity.

FUSE

How to Combine Ideas in Surprising New Ways

> Creativity is just connecting things. When you ask creative people how they did something, they feel a little guilty because they didn't really do it, they just saw something. It seemed obvious to them after a while. That's because they were able to connect experiences they've had and synthesize new things. And the reason they were able to do that was that they've had more experiences than other people.
>
> **Steve Jobs**

In 1993 a small, unknown company with the strange name, Wizards of the Coast, released a new card game called *Magic: The Gathering*. In 1994 Magic made $40 million. In 1995 customers collected more than five hundred million cards. One of the most successful new games ever, *Magic* had quickly become a gaming epidemic.

What made *Magic* different from every other card game? Simple: each deck contains sixty cards, but every deck is different—the company has made thousands of different cards, and every deck contains a unique assortment. When you get together with someone else to play, you can choose any sixty cards out of all the cards you've purchased. This encourages players to keep buying new decks to increase their potential weapons; most players have hundreds of cards, and some have thousands.

Because the company makes sure some cards are rarer than others, players often trade to get cards they like but don't have. It's like collecting baseball cards in the old days—and that's not by accident. Inventor Richard Garfield's genius was to fuse two concepts that had never been combined before: card game plus collectible items. The game succeeded because it incorporated all of the features we normally associate with collectibles: it created a community of shared interest in which fans of the game can talk endlessly about rare and favorite cards, and can search avidly for those they desire. With the success of *Magic*, Garfield's fusion spawned an entire new game genre called "trading card games."

The discipline of fusing is behind many great ideas:

- *Reese's candy*: peanut butter + chocolate
- *Rollerblading*: ice skating + roller skating
- *MTV*: music + television
- *Drive-in banking*: car + banking
- *Printing press*: wine press + coin punch

Brain science is just now beginning to reveal how the mind uses fusion to generate new ideas. In a recent study, British neuroscientist Paul Howard-Jones conducted a fascinating experiment in which he elicited creativity in the laboratory with a simple task. First, he asked people to invent a story using three words. Half of the participants got words that were pretty closely related, such as "brush," "teeth," and "shine." He told them to "be uncreative" with their story, and they obeyed:

> The children were told that they must **brush** their **teeth** when they are young in order to make them **shine** and that they wouldn't have any friends if their teeth weren't shiny. So every single night, the children brushed their teeth to make them shine.

The other half got words that had nothing in common, like "cow," "zip," and "star." Howard-Jones told them to be as creative as they possibly could. These stories, not surprisingly, were a lot more creative, as they zigged and zagged all over the place:

> This cow got so fed up with people doubting that **cows** could jump over the moon that it decided to jump over a **star**. To do this, it wore a special rocket suit. The cow **zipped** up the space suit, lit the blue touch paper and flew up over the star.

Howard-Jones then added in another twist: for the related words, he asked people to try to be creative. For example, one person came up with this creative story with the related words "kick," "football," and "goal":

> Marooned on a desert island with nothing to do I **kicked** around watermelons. I became so good at it that, when I was finally picked up by a passing boat, I was encouraged to join the local **football** team—I scored lots of **goals** and was soon recognized for the amazing talent that I'd become.

Then, for the unrelated words, he asked people to be uncreative. Someone came up with this uncreative story with the unrelated words "cloud," "strike," and "grapes":

> I looked at the sky on a really dark day not so long ago—it was really black and one particular **cloud** looked as though there was lightning going to come out of it. The **strike** just happened then and it hit the bunch of **grapes** I was eating at the same time—not me.

Which stories ended up being the most creative? Does it matter if the words are related or not, or is it more important that you're trying to be creative? A panel of five judges rated the creativity of the stories on a scale of one to five. The five judges agreed over 80 percent of the time, and their ratings were averaged for each story.

The results: when you create a story from unrelated words, it's significantly more creative than when you use related words. The researchers found that combining unrelated words results in increased brain activation of several regions associated with problem solving and higher thought, including the anterior cingulate cortex and the frontal medial gyrus.

Then they explored further, asking, "Does it matter if you're trying to be creative or not?" Their most surprising finding was that even when people with unrelated words were trying to be uncreative, their stories were still judged to be *more creative* than the deliberately creative stories told with related words!

If you start with unrelated things, you're almost guaranteed to be more creative.

The message is that if you start with unrelated things, you're almost guaranteed to be more creative—even if you're not setting out to be.

You can try this experiment yourself right now: write a story, about four or five sentences long, that uses the three words that follow. Don't take any more than one or two minutes. Try to be as creative as possible.

Flea   Sing   Sword

These are unrelated words, so coming up with a creative story is relatively easy—almost inevitable. There's just no obvious way these three words go together.

Now, try to be as creative as possible as you write a story with these three words:

Magician   Trick   Rabbit

This is much harder! To make it creative, you have to reject the obvious story that immediately presents itself. You have to reformulate the problem so you can find some way in which the words are not automatically related.

This research is a convincing demonstration of the power of fusing: combining things that don't normally belong together results in greater creativity.

The Practices

The first five steps lead to a steady stream of small ideas, the real wellspring of creativity. The next step is to bounce these ideas together, to see which ones make interesting and useful combinations. The techniques in this chapter help you combine ideas in ways that are more likely to lead to great ideas like *Magic: The Gathering*. Fusing involves mastering three practices: Force-Fuse, Make Analogies, and Do a People Mash-Up.

The First Practice of Fusing: Force-Fuse

The three techniques of this first practice enhance your ability to combine ideas that don't naturally go together. Combining similar ideas or objects tends to result in obvious creations, and these tend to be less creative. For example, combining chocolate and peanut butter gets you a new candy, the Reese's Peanut Butter Cup; but both chocolate and peanut butter are snack foods, so Reese's candies are delicious but not very surprising.

Let's try to combine two very different things: What do you get when you combine a potato chip and a magazine?

Most people are stumped by this kind of challenge—it's not at all obvious what the combination would look like. But as we just saw with the Paul Howard-Jones study, psychological research shows that if you can think of a combination, it's guaranteed to be more surprising than combining peanut butter and chocolate. Is it a magazine that comes packed with a bag of chips? Is it a magazine with edible pages, so you can eat it when you're done reading it? Maybe this combination would have led you to invent

Pringles Prints, potato chips that have cute little jokes printed on them with an edible vegetable-based dye. Now *that's* a surprising creation.

At the outset, these distant combinations are brainteasers—when you attempt to fuse ideas across a great distance, they have no apparent relationship to get you started. These three techniques ready you for the challenge; using them, you'll hone your ability to combine all sorts of ideas, no matter how distant and incongruous they seem.

 Make Remote Associations

Throughout most of human history, access to the written word was a privilege reserved for the wealthy. Only moneyed families could afford to hire tutors to teach their children to read, and books were incredibly expensive. This all changed around 1440, when Johannes Gutenberg perfected the first printing press in Germany. Gutenberg's printing press made it possible to publish books hundreds of times faster than monks could copy them. The cost of a book dropped dramatically as a result, and soon ordinary people all over Europe could afford books.

Gutenberg invented his revolutionary printing press by fusing two radically different technologies. The first was the wine press—a flat, round plate on top of a vat of grapes, with a screw and crank on top of that. You turn the crank, and the screw pushes the plate down into the vat, squeezing the juice out of the grapes. The second technology was the coin punch—a piece of hard metal with the coin's image raised up, so that when it's pressed into a softer metal, the image becomes embedded. Gutenberg's key insight was that each letter would be its own "coin punch" and that you could construct a line of text by lining up these letter punches in a row—what we call *moveable type*. A sheet of paper is inserted in the machine, and the "wine press" is cranked down to impress the letters onto the page.

Gutenberg's invention is a famous example of a *distant associa-tion*—a combination of very different ideas. What could be more different from making wine than punching coins?

Here's a simple game to help you master this ability. Pick up the book closest to you right now (not this book!). Turn to page 56. Find the fifth sentence.

Pick up a second book, ideally on a very different topic. Again, turn to page 56 and find the fifth sentence.

The Sun Tracker beach chair solves a common sunbathing problem: with an ordinary beach chair, every thirty minutes or so, you have to get up and turn your chair to follow the sun. The design firm IDEO combined the beach chair with a computer monitor's ball-and-socket swivel stand to create a beach chair that allows you to turn to face the sun with only a tiny push of your feet.

Now you're ready for the challenge: tell a story that reveals a connection between these two sentences. Sometimes it will turn out to be fairly easy, but usually the sentences will be completely unrelated, and by zig zagging between them to create a meaningful narrative, you are practicing forming distant associations.

The "page 56" game is a variant of a meme that people were emailing around the Internet in 2008. After receiving a "What's on page 56?" message, each person would post the fifth sentence from a book's page 56 on a blog or as a Facebook status update. I combined—fused—this 2008 fad with a common improv theater game called "First Line, Last Line." The actors ask the audience to suggest two lines of dialogue; the first line is spoken to start the scene, and then the actors have to create a believable dramatic scene that leads logically to the last line of dialogue.

This game, like Howard-Jones's creativity experiments, exercises your ability to create distant connections. It has quite a few variations; here are five more:

- *Grid the combinations (variation 1).* Pick a page of a book at random and write down the first word on the page. Do this with six different pages to get six random words. Then arrange them on a piece of paper as three row names and three column names to form a three-by-three grid. Then, for each of the nine cells of the grid, combine its row and column name and describe the combination.

- *Chain the associations (variation 2).* Pick two words at random from anywhere you like—magazines, books, junk mail, or the world list in Chapter Five. Then create a chain of associations that links them. After you create one chain, come up with a completely different chain using the same two words. Keep going until you've created five different associative chains between your two words. (The later chains will probably have more total words than your first ones.)

- *Find a random trigger (variation 3).* When you're stumped trying to solve a specific problem, pick a random page of a book and look at the first word on the page. Now force yourself to think of at least five ideas related to your problem that are based on this word.

- *Connect more words (variation 4).* The list on pages 137–139 of Chapter Five is filled with words that are good for forced connections. Close your eyes and put your finger down any one of the three pages twice to identify two random words. Then think of all of the possible connections.

- *Make it a game (variation 5).* Do this one in a group. Have each person think of a common object that starts with the same letter as his or her name. Then pair everyone up and ask each pair to invent a combination of their two objects and describe it to the group.

Sharper

Here's a problem I face every day: to gain access to the parking garage on my university campus, I have to reach out the window and swipe my ID card. The problem is that I keep my ID card in my wallet, which is usually in my pocket. So I take out the wallet, remove the ID card, set the wallet on the seat next to me, swipe the ID card, and then put the ID card on top of the wallet while I drive around looking for a parking space. And here's the problem: I often get out of the car and walk to my office leaving my wallet lying on the seat.

I decided to use variation 4, "find a random trigger." When I opened a nearby book, the first word was "sharper." Here are some ideas inspired by that word:

1. If my ID card had sharp edges, it would cut my finger each time I used it and the lingering pain would help remind me about the wallet on the seat.

2. I could use a sharp pair of scissors to cut out the narrow strip that scans, and keep that strip in my pocket (or on a bungee cord around my neck, if my wife didn't send the fashion police after me).

3. If the wallet were sharper, it would be thinner, and I could fit it in my front shirt pocket instead of putting it on the seat. Or I could buy a thin wallet with an outside pocket for my ID.

4. If my brain were sharper, as in smarter, I wouldn't forget. And if the university were sharper, it might issue a separate parking card I could keep in the car.

Your turn. Can you think of a fifth possibility?

 Combine Concepts

Select one of these imaginary objects and draw what it might look like:

- A piece of furniture that is also a kind of fruit
- A vehicle that is also a kind of fish

- A type of food that is also a kind of rock
- A fruit that is also a kind of human dwelling
- A food flavoring that is also a kind of tool
- A computer that is also a kind of teacup
- A cooking stove that is also a kind of bicycle
- A lampshade that is also a kind of book

These imaginary objects were used by psychologist James Hampton to study our ability to form creative combinations. Hampton found that everyone can do this, and most people display great creativity—even though there are many different, sometimes opposing, ways to creatively solve the problem. With "a piece of furniture that is also a kind of fruit," the main challenge is that fruit is perishable and furniture is durable. Some people imagined a durable fruit; others imagined a piece of furniture that rotted away. With "a fruit that is also a kind of human dwelling," one person imagined the core of the fruit hollowed out to form a spiral staircase. With "a cooking stove that is also a kind of bicycle," one person imagined the bike's tubes filled with steam that is released to do the cooking; another person imagined that pedaling the bike provided the energy to power the stove.

This technique works because it forces you to stretch and bend your mind's most stable and embedded concepts—objects you've lived with your entire life, like fruit and furniture and books.

 Cook on All Burners

When Mihaly Csikszentmihalyi interviewed ninety-six exceptional creators about their work habits, he found that they shared a common practice: they all worked on more than one project at a time. This was true of scientists, artists, writers, and dancers—creators in all fields. Having more than one project under way means that if you reach an impasse on one project, you can just shift gears and move on to another project for a while, then come back later. And it turns out that some of the best ideas come from combining ideas across multiple projects.

Take a lesson from the exceptional creators and always have multiple projects in progress. Every week or so, give yourself some time to step back and think about potential connections between your different projects.

Why not apply the three techniques of Force-Fuse to your idea log? Get in the habit of going back through your idea log and combining different observations and ideas. Make sure to force connections between material that seems completely unrelated—don't focus on the obvious connections.

Or, apply this practice to your idea box. Recall (from Chapter Three) that an idea box is a container in which you store interesting objects, photos, and news articles. When you're stumped for an idea, open up the box and remove one or two things at random. See what happens if you combine them.

The Second Practice of Fusing: Make Analogies

The preceding techniques are mostly exercises that you can use on a regular basis to enhance your creative potential. The following techniques are designed to be applied to a specific problem or creative challenge.

Psychologists have discovered that many great new ideas result from *analogy*, defined as a similarity in structure between two objects or concepts that have very different surface features. Recent experiments have revealed a lot about how the mind engages in "analogical thinking." Brain imaging studies show that analogical thinking fires up the anterior superior temporal gyrus in the right hemisphere, the same area that's implicated in studies of the proverbial flash of insight.

You think by analogy when your mind notices a particular property in its *target* and then finds the same property in a *source*.

You can then use the source to help explain that property of the target. In the analogy "Sound is like water waves," for example, *sound* is the target and *water waves* is the source that's helping you explain how sound moves.

The three techniques of this practice help you fuse ideas to create analogies.

Synectics

Analogical thinking was the core practice of the famous 1960s consulting firm Synectics. Its very name refers to the joining of different and apparently irrelevant elements. Here's an example: a Synectics group was tasked with inventing a new kind of energy-saving roof, one that could change from white in the summer (to reflect the hot sun) to black in the winter (to absorb the sun's rays). One group member proposed an analogy: he knew of a species of flounder that could change from white to black depending on the color of the sea floor (white for sand, black for mud). The magic is that the flounder's outer skin is white, but underneath are tiny black chromatophores that are pushed to the skin's surface when the flounder finds itself against a darker muddy sea floor. Using analogy, the group proposed a new kind of roofing material that's black, but with tiny white plastic balls buried underneath. When the roof gets hot, the white balls expand and pop through the black surface.

 Use Direct Analogy

First, pick an item from one of the categories in the list that follows. Or pick an object in your house or outdoors.

- *Countries*: England, Russia, Japan, Brazil, New Zealand, Portugal, Costa Rica

- *Animals*: ostrich, dog, monkey, earthworm
- *Sports and hobbies*: football (ball, net); cricket (bat, wicket, ball); billiards (cue stick, table); stamp collecting (book, transparent envelope); needlepoint (needle, thread, cloth)
- *Tools*: eggbeater, saw, scissors, drill, pump

Now, write down five characteristics of that object.

Finally, look at each of the five characteristics in turn, and think creatively about ways to apply that characteristic to your problem.

This technique works best if you focus on the underlying structure of the source (the characteristics you've chosen), and then apply it to the underlying structure of your target, which is your creative challenge. Unfortunately, psychologists have discovered, our natural tendency is to focus on surface features rather than underlying structure. So when you're writing down five characteristics of your source object, avoid listing superficial features. For example, if you picked the saw, don't write down characteristics like "sharp" or "made of metal." Instead, think of underlying structural properties—not what a particular saw happens to be made of, but how all saws function. "Cuts by moving back and forth" would be a structural characteristic; so would "requires pressure downward to cut" or "sometimes gets stuck in whatever material it is cutting."

The best sources for this technique are objects that are far removed from your actual problem. You'll also want to choose something of a very different size and scale than your prob-lem. For example, if you're faced with a vast, abstract spiritual problem, then choose something very tiny, like an earthworm or a sewing needle. (Remember the camel trying to pass into the kingdom of God through the eye of a needle?) Inversely, if you have a creative challenge with your needlepoint, choose something very large, like Russia, or a huge piece of construction equipment.

Mimic Nature

We just learned how Synectics invented a new energy-saving roof by copying a fish. And in Chapter Three we learned how George de Mestral got the inspiration for Velcro fasteners by closely observing how burrs attached themselves to his dog's fur. These stories show us the power of *biomimicry*—a form of analogy that starts from nature.

Biomimicry takes advantage of nature's wisdom, borrowing from solutions that have emerged over thousands of years of evolution. Why reinvent the wheel when nature's solution is already out there?

- Sonar, used in submarines and other marine vessels, was inspired by the way whales and dolphins navigate in water, and how bats use echolocation to find their way in the dark.
- Architect Mick Pearce designed a self-cooling building inspired by termite mounds.

As with all creative analogy, the challenge is to stay focused on the underlying structure of nature's solution, rather than its superficial features. If de Mestral had only looked at the obvious surface features, he would have thought of burrs as sharp, painful, and annoying—and none of those characteristics is likely to result in creative inspiration!

 Use Personal Analogy

This technique is easier than it at first sounds: you imagine yourself "inside" the problem. A few examples might make the method clearer:

- A paper company asked its staff to imagine what it would be like to be the tree that's going through processing.
- Scientists who were developing a reflective window imagined themselves as the molecules of the glass. From the perspective of those molecules, they asked, "What would happen to us that might make us reflective?"

- Albert Einstein famously imagined that he was a beam of light, and imagined what would happen to time and space if he viewed them from that perspective—moving at the speed of light. This thought experiment led to his theory of special relativity.

- In designing a new online bank, the staff imagined they were a bill, traveling from the electric company to the customer and ultimately being paid.

- A researcher imagined he was a mosquito and wondered how he would survive rainfall, given that each raindrop that fell on him would be the equivalent of a comet plummeting down on his head. Further study revealed that mosquitoes hitch rides on raindrops! And they nearly always survive because of it.

Imagine you are your product. If you're a tax accountant, imagine what the tax form sees as the client tries to decipher it. If you're a dairy farmer, imagine what it's like for your cows to move through the milking facility. If you're a manufacturer, how does your product feel at each moment during its life span? Is it awkward as it leaves the factory? Is it nervous rattling around in the truck because its packaging isn't secure? Is it afraid the customer will get mad trying to find its model number to fill out the warranty form? Imagine the complete life span of your product, from manufacture to being recycled—where will it go?—or discarded.

The Third Practice of Fusing: Do a People Mash-Up

Fuse your ideas with those of someone very different. What better way to find a distant combination? The three techniques of this practice help you exercise your ability to be inspired by very different people.

Talk to Someone Different

Scientists in the 1950s knew that each cell contained DNA, the genetic code that carries the information necessary to create a human being. But no one knew *how* DNA conveyed its orders. If scientists could figure out the structure of DNA, they'd be one step closer to learning how it worked its magic.

The insight came from a people mash-up: a diverse team including a biologist, an X-ray crystallographer, and a physicist (James Watson, Maurice Wilkins, and Francis Crick, respectively). This diversity resulted in distant combinations, and that's what allowed them to beat other top research teams working on the same problem. They even beat the leading contender: Nobel Prize winner Linus Pauling, somebody everyone had expected to be the first to discover DNA's structure.

When was the last time you talked, seriously and at length, to someone thirty years older? Or thirty years younger?

We spend time with people like us because it keeps us in our comfort zone. But diverse concepts don't usually clash in a comfort zone; they're too busy clinging to their comfort. Stretch your zone: practice talking to people who think differently and see the world differently. When was the last time you talked, seriously and at length, to someone thirty years older? Or thirty years younger? Pose your problem to someone in her eighties. Talk to a child about what games are cool these days.

Imagine yourself as someone different for one day, and try to see things as if you were that person. A chef might pass an empty storefront and see it as a potential location for a new restaurant. A foreign student passing the same empty storefront might be shocked that the U.S. economy allows businesses to fail, and then realize that this "creative destruction" is the driving force of our economic success. A building inspector, meanwhile, will be worrying about kids exploring the abandoned space and getting hurt.

Superhero

A variation of this exercise is to imagine yourself as a famous superhero from the comics or the movies. At the start of the day, make a list of the unique characteristics of that superhero, and then imagine yourself seeing the world as that superhero for the entire day. For example, if you're Spiderman, you'll see tall buildings as places to attach your spiderweb, to help you swing quickly through the air.

How would this superhero solve your creative challenge? The solutions a superhero comes up with might seem wild and crazy; but remember, you're going for distant, remote combinations. Just jot them down; practical modifications can come later.

You might also imagine yourself as a famous creator from a different field. How would Einstein structure a novel? Would he show the same event from ten different perspectives? Would he collapse time? How would architect Frank Lloyd Wright design a nonprofit program for teens? Around a central fireplace, no doubt, with all details to human scale and carefully proportioned, and with an emphasis on individual craftsmanship.

 Crash a Meeting

Attend a group meeting or an event that you've never been to before. (Choose a meeting that's open to the public, of course—unless you want to challenge yourself by comparing perspectives during a night in jail!)

Try a Toastmasters meeting, your local school board's monthly meeting, or your town's monthly public meeting. Try going to an art opening, a concert, or an opening ceremony for a new business or restaurant.

Wherever you go, observe closely; notice everything. Take notes, if you can do so without being too conspicuous, and write down even the obvious things people do. Are they sitting down?

Standing up? Do they seem to know each other? Are they happy, tense, or bored? What do they care about? What excites them? What angers them?

 Work in the Intersection

Many of the companies known for their high level of innovation are building office design layouts that lead people to unexpected encounters in hallways or common spaces. Franz Johansson, author of *The Medici Effect*, refers to these spaces as the "intersection," and they drive creativity because these unexpected encounters are more likely to result in surprising new ideas.

Steelcase, a one-hundred-year-old American furniture company that is reinventing the future of work, built a Corporate Development Center designed to increase the likelihood that people will bump into useful strangers. They call their design principle "functional inconvenience," because the floor layout deliberately slows everyone down, with the goal of increasing creative conversations between people who normally wouldn't run into each other.

The Seattle headquarters of the Bill & Melinda Gates Foundation is designed with fewer private offices and more collaboration space. Stairways are inviting—open to the rooms and filled with natural light—because so many chance encounters happen on the stairs. And the stairways end at a coffee station or at an informal grouping of furniture, so it's easy to sit down if you want to continue that unexpected conversation. Many work spaces are out in the open—there are tables in atriums and alcoves next to walkways.

In Grand Rapids, Michigan, the new Grid70 work space is designed to encourage workers to move around freely, to bounce ideas off of each other. Companies that have rented space there include Steelcase, Wolverine, Meijer, and Amway.

Steven Johnson, author of *Where Good Ideas Come From*, opened a TED talk by describing the first coffeehouse to open in England. That coffeehouse played a significant role in the birth of the Enlightenment. "Chance favors the connected mind," as Johnson likes to say, and when all different kinds of people drink and talk together, there's a lively, happy chaos in which good ideas come readily.

The message is: don't work alone all day in your office. Even if you work in an old-style cubicle farm, inside a big office tower, here are some ways you can spend time in the intersection:

- Instead of getting coffee from the machine on your floor, go up or down a level and linger by a different coffee machine. Make a point of saying hello to each person you meet; introduce yourself and say what you do. Chances are pretty good others will be happy to meet you, and might even have a question that only you can answer.

- Don't get lunch every day with the same coworkers; introduce yourself to a group of strangers in the company lunchroom and ask if you can join them. Again, make sure to say what you do. Ask about their work and look for connections with your own projects.

- Chance encounters often happen when people are walking or standing up, so if you have some reading to do, leave your desk. Read while standing in a hallway; find a comfy seat in a lobby, atrium, or foyer; or hang out in the mail room or coffee room. Make sure to look up and greet people who pass by.

It might be harder to introduce yourself if you're a bit introverted, but you can still put yourself in a place where encounters are more likely. Once you do, there's an excellent chance you'll meet people who are more extroverted, and they'll take it from there.

Onward . . .

You've completed the first six steps. You've identified a great problem, you've gathered all of the relevant information, and you have an amazing collection of surprising new ideas. Now you need the final two steps to turn your creative inspiration into reality. First, you need to choose—to apply critical evaluation to your ideas. And then you need to make your idea into a concrete reality.

THE SEVENTH STEP
CHOOSE

How to Pick the Best Ideas and Then Make Them Even Better

> Creativity is allowing yourself to make mistakes. Art is knowing which ones to keep.
>
> **Scott Adams, cartoonist, in *The Dilbert Principle***

To be creative, you have to generate boatloads of ideas. To be creative successfully, you have to let most of them sink, because the real genius lies in picking good ideas. Today's symphony orchestras play only about 35 percent of Johann Sebastian Bach's, Wolfgang Amadeus Mozart's, or Ludwig van Beethoven's compositions—which means these composers have a pretty low success rate! The rest of us, realistically, can't hope to do any better. And yet if you fail most of the time at your job, you won't stay employed very long. I'm a college teacher, and if even 50 percent of my students failed to learn, I'd get fired for incompetence.

What if 90 percent of your company's products fail? It will surely go out of business. But you'll often hear people say that innovative companies "embrace failure." How do they stay in business? They stay because they've figured out how to transform failure into learning, so they can keep moving forward.

Consider W. L. Gore. You know the company for its famous waterproof fabric, Gore-Tex. But you might not know that

Gore is an innovation powerhouse, responsible for hundreds of products in fifteen different industry sectors, from sports to music to medical devices. The company succeeds because its employees are masters of choosing.

Dave Myer, an engineer in one of Gore's plants in Flagstaff, Arizona, invented Gore's Ride On brand of bike cables. The wire cables are coated with an invisibly thin layer of plastic—something like Teflon—that let the gears shift more smoothly. But Myer had a hunch that this new "coated wire" technology might be useful for other products. He started looking around, casually, for a new application. One day he had to suffer through a kid's birthday party at Chuck E. Cheese's. As he watched the animated robots play and sing, the idea came to him: Gore's plastic-coated wires could be used to invent a new type of puppet control cable. Myer raced home, got some old, used guitar strings from a neighbor, and coated them with Gore's plastic. He was thrilled with the result, and he envisioned selling his cables to theme parks all over the world.

> There is no such thing as a failed experiment, only experiments with unexpected outcomes.
>
> R. Buckminster Fuller

Six months later—half a year of skipped meals and late nights and working on weekends—Myer forced himself to admit that his idea wasn't so good after all. Puppets didn't really perform noticeably better with the new cables, and the potential market wasn't big enough to make money, anyway. He'd failed.

In those months he spent slaving away on puppet cables, though, he'd coated a lot of used guitar strings. As he contemplated his slick pile of coated strings, a new thought came to him: maybe, now that they were coated smooth, they could be used on a guitar again. . .

Jackpot! This time, Myer was right. His technology had the potential to solve an age-old problem that plagues every guitarist. Musicians love the bright and resonant sound of new guitar strings, but after just a few days of playing, oils and microscopic flecks of dead skin become embedded in the coils of the strings, and the sound starts to dull. Guitarists who play a lot have to replace their strings every couple of weeks. Myer realized that if the strings were coated with an invisible plastic layer, it might keep them sounding bright and new indefinitely. So he chose *this* idea.

He chose right. Soon after its release in 1997, Gore's new brand of strings—Elixir—became the top-selling acoustic guitar string in the United States. Myer had zig zagged his way to a brilliant new product.

The story shows the importance of choosing. First, Myer had to be receptive to the possibility that his puppet control

When you become a master at choosing, you instinctively recognize good ideas.

cables might not pan out. By being a master at choosing, he was able to accurately evaluate the idea sooner rather than later. (In the world of product development, six months is a couple of minutes. All too often, ideas are years past the prototype stage and well into manufacture before anyone discovers their fatal flaws.) Second, Myer had to be a master at coming up with new ways to reinterpret and reuse his first idea's underlying technology. Third, he had to be perceptive enough to choose to proceed with the guitar string idea.

Exceptional creators think differently about failure. Instead of waiting until the end of a project to judge "success or failure," they make critical decisions throughout the creative process—every minute, every day, every week. They don't get too attached to any one idea, because if they did they'd end up wasting time, continuing down a dead end simply because they were afraid to walk away from the effort already invested. When choosing is embedded in a creative life, tiny moments of failure just prompt a new direction, a zig or zag that lets you move forward again, lesson learned. With that kind of flexibility and resilience, it's easy to transform what seems to be a loss into a brilliant gain.

Just about everyone has heard of *brainstorming*, a classic technique used in groups to generate ideas. The most famous brainstorming rule is, "No criticism; the wilder the idea, the better." You're told to go for quantity of ideas, not stopping to worry about whether they're any good. The logic behind the rule is that silencing your inner critic allows more creative ideas to surface. If that's true, then choosing must just get in the way of creativity, right?

Au contraire. The latest research shows us that people generate better ideas when they're guided by clear criteria—in other words, when they're constantly choosing. One great example comes from a study by two psychology professors at Purdue. They gave three groups of students the classic brainstorming instructions: "No criticism; be wild and crazy." They told another three groups to do just the opposite: "We want good, practical ideas. Let's try to avoid stupid or silly ones. The emphasis is on quality, not quantity." In other words, these three groups were told to be *more* critical!

All six groups were asked to come up with brand names for products that would be marketed to Purdue students: a new deodorant, a new car . . . Once they'd made their list, all of the ideas were evaluated by a new group of fifty students. The professors asked students to indicate how much each brand name appealed to them, using a five-point scale to rate each name.

Guess what? The critical group, told to avoid "stupid or silly" ideas, came up with much better ideas than the freewheeling, no-criticism group. The uncritical group generated about twice as many ideas—after all, the classic brainstorming instructions tell you to emphasize quantity—but most of their additional ideas were bad ideas. Incorporating criteria into the creative process results in better ideas.

The famous design firm IDEO swears by brainstorming; the company tells its designers to go for wild ideas. But when you watch what designers actually do in a brainstorming session, for example in the famous "redesign a shopping cart" video that appeared on TV's *Nightline*, it's obvious that they always have clear criteria for what they're trying to accomplish. Before the brainstorming session starts, everyone is informed of what the goals are and what they need to accomplish by the end. One of the brainstorming rules posted on the wall is, "Stay focused, stay on topic."

In the *Nightline* video, an eclectic team of IDEO designers—with backgrounds in linguistics, psychology, biology, and business—has to improve on the familiar, classic design of a shopping cart. They keep their ideas focused within a broad set of constraints and criteria. For example, the carts have to nest together, as shopping carts do now, so they don't take up much space when they're not being used. "If it doesn't nest, we don't have a solution," the group's facilitator reminds the team at regular intervals. Another criterion is safety—they've learned that many children injure themselves every year playing or riding on shopping carts, and they are determined to design a safer shopping cart.

Even with constraints this tight, IDEO designers came up with some wonderfully strange ideas. One team member proposed "a Velcro baby seat on the cart, and then the baby can wear Velcro pants to hold him tightly." This sounds ridiculous—but even so, it's focused on the problem presented, its mechanism is easy to understand, and its special pants and seats wouldn't cost that much to make. Plus, it satisfies the design criteria. No one in the group suggested really crazy ideas, like "Have an army of flying fairies hold the baby in place" or "Give the baby a sleeping pill." The final cart had a cozy plastic baby seat (far more comfortable than the old metal one) and a rounded plastic bar that wrapped around and secured the baby in place. Better ideas result from clear criteria—from mastery of the seventh step, choose.

Real, Win, Worth

Gore has codified the act of choosing into a three-step mantra—Real, Win, Worth—that every employee can recite.

1. *Real.* Does the invention solve a customer problem?
2. *Win.* Do we have the skills we need to make this a success?
3. *Worth.* Can we make and sell this at a profit?

Let's put the Elixir guitar strings to this test.

1. *Real.* They solve a distinct, long-standing problem of dirty, muffled guitar strings.
2. *Win.* Gore is skilled at coating wires—we know that from the Ride On bike cables.
3. *Worth.* Guitarists are willing to pay three times as much for Elixir strings because these last many times longer than regular strings, and they also sound better for longer. To a musician, that bright, crisp sound is priceless.

Gore is great at the first six steps of creativity. But its employees are also masters of selection; they know how to choose the best ideas.

The Practices

The creative life is filled with new ideas. The first six steps will fill your plate with far more ideas than you can ever pursue. Now your challenge is choosing the best of them.

When you become a master at choosing, you instinctively recognize good ideas. The techniques in this chapter help you develop that sense. You'll learn to identify the most promising ideas, and to approach all ideas with a constant focus on improvement. Because you're intelligently editing and refining your ideas, you'll be able to turn potential failures into surprising successes.

It's often said that the flip side of creativity is failure; that's because only a small percentage of your many ideas will go anywhere. Choosing prepares you to transform failure into success. You will master the practice of constant editing—because every idea can be made better, with later insights and ideas that build on it.

Choosing means mastering four practices: Know What You're Looking For; Host an Idea Competition; Look Past the Good; and Edit, Revise, Improve.

The First Practice of Choosing: Know What You're Looking For

A good idea is one that's inherently interesting. It builds on previous ideas and has the power to generate all sorts of good ideas in the future; it also has the ability to combine with other ideas in intriguing ways.

How can you tell which ideas are this richly layered? Successful creators know what they're looking for because their creative judgment is honed by years of practice. Use these four techniques to help identify ideas worth pursuing.

 Train Your Intuition

Powerful creative solutions are gorgeous: they have that symmetry and completeness and perfect form we recognize as beauty. "When I am working on a problem, I never think about beauty," said R. Buckminster Fuller. "But when I have finished, if the solution is not beautiful, I know it is wrong." Fuller was a visionary architect, and we're used to thinking about beauty in the visual arts, so his way of working isn't that surprising. But physicists and mathematicians talk just as passionately about the beauty of a good theory or formula.

To choose the most creative solution, you have to learn to trust the beauty you sense in a good idea. Train your intuition by finding examples—creative solutions you admire—and studying them. What is it that makes this solution so successful? Why do you like it so much? What is pleasing about it? What sets it apart?

Rigorous reasoning can sometimes lead you to focus too much on potential problems, like the million ways that an idea could go wrong. When you rely on well-trained intuition, you're more able to see an idea's hidden potential—and hidden beauty. The problem with *untrained* intuition is that it often responds most strongly to the familiar, the comfortable. If you're stumped and need a truly creative solution, you can't always count on your gut to choose. That's why it helps to have a list of explicit criteria— like Gore's Real, Win, Worth. Come up with your own criteria, and begin to use them.

The rest of the techniques in this chapter are designed to help you avoid the pitfalls of intuition. As you begin to master these techniques, you'll get better at identifying beautiful creativity.

 Color Your Choices

Here's a way to sort through a lot of ideas quickly. First, take out a blank piece of paper and draw a big square. Divide the square into four quadrants.

Then, along the top of the square, write "normal and ordinary" on the left; write "original and breakthrough" on the right. Along the left side of the square, write "highly feasible and useful" at the top; write "difficult and of unclear use" at the bottom.

	Normal and ordinary ideas	Original and breakthrough ideas
Highly feasible and useful	BLUE	GREEN!
Difficult and of unclear use	RED	YELLOW

Now, put each of your ideas into one of the four quadrants, using a different colored pen for each quadrant:

- *Not-so-original ideas that are highly feasible (upper left).* These will be ideas that require an effective and efficient implementation plan. (Blue)
- *Very original ideas that are not feasible (bottom right).* These ideas will have to have really high potential to be selected. (Yellow)
- *Very original ideas that are highly feasible (top right).* Jackpot! Start working on these ideas right away. (Green)
- *Not-so-original ideas that are not feasible (bottom left).* Rarely will you generate an idea like this. If you do, throw it out immediately. (Red)

If you're doing this in a group, you can use this technique after a brainstorming session has generated tons of ideas, and they're all displayed on a whiteboard, poster paper, or sticky notes on the wall. Ask everyone to vote by tagging each idea with a blue, yellow, green, or red sticker.

 Go for Simple, Elegant, Robust

No matter what the field, creative solutions are invariably as simple as they can be and still solve the problem; they are elegant in their design; and they are robust, rather than temporary, fragile, fickle, or frail. Apple's products are legendary because they embody these three principles so well, but the same criteria will apply to any creative solution you come up with. When you choose your idea, check it right away to see whether it realizes these three principles.

- *Simplicity.* The design expresses the essence of the problem, paring it down to the core. Your solution is direct and efficient, and it's not complicated by anything unnecessary. As Albert Einstein famously said, "Everything should be made as simple as possible, but not simpler."

  A scientist described a process of creativity that goes through three phases: "We start off with the simple hypothesis, our experimentation leads to more and more complex hypotheses, and in the end, we make our discovery, which is profoundly simple." Designers report a remarkably similar process. The famous designer John Maeda described design as "starting simple, then getting complex, and ending up as simple as possible."

- *Elegance.* Elegance means doing the most with the least—finding solutions so ingeniously simple, they take your breath away. For example, Morse code uses a unique sequence of dots and dashes to send each letter down a wire. It's much more elegant than some earlier ideas, such as the idea of having twenty-six wires, one corresponding to each letter.

- *Robustness.* Robust designs continue to work, even under adverse conditions or when they're used incorrectly. Because of this resilience, they are sometimes said to "fail gracefully." The obvious way to get robustness is to make something very strong, so that it's almost impossible to break. But that's expensive, big, and bulky. A more creative robustness comes from adaptable and flexible design. A great example is shatterproof windshield glass. It breaks, but it doesn't send shards of glass into the passenger compartment. Graceful failure.

The Internet has the same quality: it's robust because its "packet-switching" design allows information to travel in many different ways from source to destination. If one pathway is destroyed, many other routes are available. And any "classic masterpiece" of art or drama or literature is robust, too: its deepest meanings are so universal, so true and timeless, that they endure for centuries.

 Check Your Ideas

This technique helps bring you back to the nuts and bolts, and it's particularly useful in a business setting, or with a technical invention. Try to answer these questions about each of your ideas:

- What need does the idea satisfy?
- If there is no present need for this idea, is there a way to spark a need?
- What are the idea's benefits?
- What is your competition? Is your idea clearly better? How will you prevent others from stealing your idea as soon as it is successful?
- What will your idea cost to implement? Will the benefits outweigh the cost?
- Do you have the resources—money, expertise, connections—to translate the idea into reality?
- If not, is there a way to acquire the resources you need?
- Is there a current market for this idea? Can your potential customers afford it? Will they buy it?

- How good is your timing? Is now the right time for this idea?
- How would you market it?

Many companies distill this list down to three simple questions quite similar to those associated with Gore's Real, Win, Worth:

1. Is there a market for it?
2. Can we do it (or make it)?
3. Can we make money at it?

 Define Greatness

Every creative challenge has its own distinct set of characteristics. The criteria I've been discussing up to this point are broad and general; you might want to get more specific when you define what counts as a great idea in your domain.

For example, if you're inventing a new board game, the characteristics of a great idea might be

- Fun
- Not too expensive
- Easy to learn

If you're trying to figure out where to go to meet new people, your list might start like this:

Board game maker Cranium created its own word to define greatness, "CHIFF" (clever, high quality, innovative, friendly, fun).

- Not too far from my house
- Not too expensive
- Involving something I enjoy doing
- Easy to enter and leave without feeling awkward

When you're making this list, a lot of the criteria will seem pretty obvious—so obvious you might feel kind of dumb writing them down. Do it anyway! Write down even the most obvious qualities of greatness. The key is to make your criteria explicit—you won't believe how much that helps when you're trying to choose the really great ideas.

The senior leadership at Virgin—the parent company of Virgin Records, Virgin Books, and Virgin Airways—will enter almost any new business as long as it meets their criteria for greatness. The idea must

- Challenge existing rules
- Provide a better consumer experience
- Be more fun
- "Put a thumb in the eye of the complacent incumbents"

The Second Practice of Choosing: Host an Idea Competition

After going through the first six steps, you'll have tons of creative ideas, more than you can ever pursue. To choose the best idea, it helps to focus on two or more ideas at once. Let your ideas compete—and may the best one win!

Look for Differences

Select any two of your ideas. Look for the differences between the ideas. Even two ideas that seem almost the same will have at least some small, subtle difference. Focus on that difference and ask yourself: "How is this important?"

Map the Grid

Start by using the earlier technique, Define Greatness. Take the list of specific criteria that you generated using this technique, and write them across the top of the page, each one at the top of its own column. If you have a bunch, it might help to turn the paper sideways to fit in more columns. If you're using a computer, you can do this with a spreadsheet in Microsoft Excel.

Ask yourself: "How important is each criterion?" Give each one a number between one and ten, with ten being really important.

Then list all of your ideas down the left side of the page, from top to bottom. Now you're ready to fill in the grid created by the column headings and the row names. Ask yourself how well each idea satisfies each criterion. Write down a rating between one and ten, with ten being really great.

To get the total worth of an idea, multiply the rating in each cell of the grid by the importance of the criterion that you wrote at the top of the column. Then add up all of these products. Write the total for each idea to the right of its corresponding row. (If you use formulas in Microsoft Excel, this will go much faster!) The best idea will have the biggest number.

If you're creating in a group setting, you can ask everyone to rate the ideas, and then figure out the group's average rating for each idea. Research shows that groups select better and more creative ideas than people working solo. There are software tools available, called "group support systems," that automatically tally everyone's ratings. But there's a cheap and easy way, too: write all of the ideas on a whiteboard, and then have each person vote by using colored sticky notes: green for an awesome idea, yellow for an okay idea, red for a bad idea. The winner will be obvious at a glance.

 Draw an Affinity Diagram

This technique works best when you have quite a lot of ideas—fifty or more.

Write each idea on its own sticky note, and stick each one up on a wall or a whiteboard with plenty of space between ideas. Or you can write them on index cards and lay them out on the floor or on a big conference table.

Look for ideas that are related to each other. When you see a potential connection between two ideas, move them so that they're closer together. As you keep rearranging ideas, a small number of idea clusters will start to emerge.

Stop as soon as all of your ideas are in clusters, and you're pretty comfortable with the groupings. Now, for each cluster in turn:

1. Identify what all the ideas in this cluster have in common, and give the cluster a name.

2. Look for interesting differences among ideas in the cluster—for example, maybe they all vary along a single dimension of contrast. In one workshop I asked the participants to list all of the groups and teams they had ever been a part of—whether in sports, volunteer activities, or the workplace. After they grouped their Post-it notes, we noticed a key dimension: the groups varied in degree of structure, ranging from informal and loose (like a group of roommates) to highly formal and organized (like an engineering project team).

This technique also works great in a group—where it's best to have each idea on a sticky note on a wall, with people walking around as they move the notes.

The Third Practice of Choosing: Look Past the Good

After you've selected a great idea, you're excited! All you can think about is how great it will be. The problem is, sometimes that excitement can blind you to weaknesses of the idea. These techniques force you to look at an idea from all sides, to notice both the good and the bad, and to use that perspective to see the bigger picture and improve the idea so it's even better.

Consider Pros and Cons

Here's a variant of a classic technique. Start by dividing a sheet of paper down the middle. The left-hand side is "Pro," and the right-hand side is "Con." Take a few minutes to write down all of the positives of the idea on the left; then take another few minutes to list all of the negatives on the right.

Then go back through both lists and assign a number, one through ten, indicating how important each pro or con is. Add up the numbers in each column, and write the total at the bottom. If the idea is a good one, the total on the left should be much higher than the total on the right.

PMI

PMI, which stands for "pluses, minuses, and interesting aspects" of a new idea, is a simple but powerful extension of the pros and cons technique. Listing the pluses and minuses is usually the easy part. But you're going to add a third column at the right of your sheet of paper, for "interesting aspects." That's where you'll focus your energy, because if your idea is interesting, it can lead to further creative thinking, idea improvement, and, later, follow-up ideas.

You can use PMI with a long list of ideas, too. Use symbols to tag each idea as great, not great, or interesting: "+" for great, "−" for not great, and "!" for interesting. Again, focus more attention on the interesting ideas than on the great ones.

 Find the Worst-Case Scenario

What unexpected, horrible things might happen? To make sure you've explored all possibilities, be as creative and broad as you can—even thinking of worst-case scenarios that are really crazy, and that you're positive will never happen. Then think of a possible sequence of events that might in fact lead to that crazy, impossible scenario.

Psychologist Gary Klein calls this a "premortem." Project yourself one year into the future, and imagine that your idea has been a total disaster. Now list all of the possible causes of the failure. This can help you see how the failure might have been avoided, thereby leading to an improvement of your idea.

The Fourth Practice of Choosing: Edit, Revise, Improve

Masters of creativity never get too attached to one idea; they don't fixate on a single vision. Even after you've selected a great idea, there's room for improvement; there always will be. Successful creativity is a way of life; the creativity never stops.

> Genius is the ability to edit.
>
> *Charlie Chaplin*

 Identify Three Benefits

Start with an idea that you're attracted to, but that you're not really sure is worth pursuing.

First, list at least three benefits of this idea. Contemplate those benefits for a few minutes each. Ask yourself if you like the idea any more than you did before. It's surprising, but research shows that it's hard to predict in advance which ideas this exercise will make you like more than you did at the outset.

Second, ask yourself what practical steps you would have to take to implement the idea. List at least three practical steps. Contemplate these three steps for a few minutes each. Ask yourself if generating these steps has made you more receptive to the idea. Just as with the first part of this technique, it's hard to predict which ideas you'll like more after completing the second part.

Research shows that about half of all ideas become more compelling as a result of this two-stage thought experiment.

Fix the Fatal Flaw

If you have lots of ideas, try this with each of them: list as many potential flaws as you can. Or, focus on one of your ideas—one that feels really great to you, but that has a fatal flaw that you just can't get past. If only you could fix that fatal flaw, you're sure you'd have a great idea. Go back to your list and look again at the other ideas, the ones that just don't seem as good. Try to force-fuse each of these other ideas with the one that has the fatal flaw. Is there some feature of a cast-off idea that might help you resolve the fatal flaw in your chosen idea?

The idea with the flaw that can be most easily overcome is the best one.

 Be the Devil's Advocate

In 1587 the Catholic Church created the position of devil's advocate. When someone is proposed to be canonized (recognized as a saint), the church appoints a lawyer, called the devil's advocate, to argue *against* canonizing the candidate. The devil's advocate is assigned the role of skeptic; for example, he or she might argue that any miracles attributed to the candidate were fraudulent or misreported. (The lawyer who supports canonization is called God's advocate.)

Be your own devil's advocate and focus on everything that's wrong with your idea.

Even better, enlist some trusted friends or colleagues to critically evaluate your idea. It helps if you have a long history of engaging in open discussions about new ideas;

Even after you've selected a great idea, there's room for improvement; there always will be. Successful creativity is a way of life; the creativity never stops.

without that history and familiarity, many people won't be honest with their criticisms. The most successful creators spend years nurturing relationships with people they can trust to be honest with them.

If you're in a group that is suffering from "groupthink"— that timid, bland mind-set in which everyone wants to get along, no one wants to rock the boat, and all decisions are unanimous—it can really help to assign someone to be the devil's advocate. That person needs a lot of confidence and has to be someone everyone in the group trusts.

Jon Citrin, CEO and founder of the Citrin Group, assigns one person to be the "Blocker" in every meeting. The Blocker's job is to disagree with everything Citrin says. The result? Serious debate, and deep consideration of the issues. And best of all, it inhibits everyone's natural instinct to always agree with the boss.

 ## Reformulate, Reuse, Reperceive

If an idea fails your tests, try to reformulate, reuse, or reperceive. This is the time to zig zag: maybe the failed idea can be used for something totally different, something unexpected. The Elixir guitar strings would never have been invented if Dave Myer had just given up after the failure of his puppet cables.

History is full of failed ideas that were later reused with great success:

- The Post-it note was a reuse of a failed adhesive, a glue that didn't stick very well.
- Thomas Edison's car battery failed because by 1909, gasoline-powered cars had taken over the market. He modified the battery and successfully sold it to factories.
- Kleenex was a reuse of a tissue originally used to remove women's face cream.

To improve the odds of successful reuse, break apart the failed idea and examine each of its components in turn. Think about how that part relates to the whole. Maybe you should remove some of the parts and save them for a future project.

Onward . . .

It's the oldest creativity advice in the book: "Silence your inner critic. Defer judgment." In the first six steps of the creative process, this can be just what you need to hear. It's especially good advice when you're just learning how to be creative. But once you have figured out how to get good ideas flowing, you *need* to judge them. The most successful creators are strong critical thinkers. They kill bad ideas early, so they don't waste a lot of time going down dead ends.

The classic advice to writers is to "kill your darlings," stripping the prose of all your favorite, invariably overwritten curlicues. Choose, refine, edit, tighten.

When I was designing video games back in the early 1980s, I spent a year working on an arcade game called *Neon*. Neon art was part of what was called the New Wave style, and *Neon* was going to be the first "New Wave" video game. The neon beams would move around the screen, changing direction randomly at ninety-degree angles. When your character flew through the air and landed on one of the beams, it changed from blue to green. If the enemy landed on your beam, it would turn red, and you'd be dead. You and your opponents were triangles (triangles were another trendy design element at the time).

Designing video games taught me many lessons about choosing. At every moment during the design, there were visual and interactive problems to be resolved, strategies to be abandoned, changes that required a play-test to see if they worked. And then, playing the game led to new zigs and zags. It always does.

Neon did well in focus tests, so we put one in an arcade for a couple of days to see if anyone would put quarters into it. The good news was that teenagers at the mall loved it. The bad news? Right at that time, the video game industry really wanted cute and furry video games—to counter a worry among parents that all video games were about shooting, war, and violence. *Neon* was the opposite of cute. After all, what could be less cuddly than a triangle? And video game manufacturers definitely had to choose carefully: only one of every ten games gets selected for production. So, sadly, *Neon* was never made.

Neon prototype, 1982.

Exceptional creators are ruthless, smashing sculptures that aren't quite right, painting over a week's worth of elaborately detailed scenery, shredding manuscripts, and taking apart inventions. They are constantly generating ideas, and then constantly examining them. In a given month, they might start fresh ten times, while more mediocre minds stick like glue to their very first idea, afraid that it's so fragile it will crumple under criticism. Real creativity is resilient. You're far more creative when you know how to choose.

MAKE

How Getting Your Ideas Out into the World Drives Creativity Forward

> Everyone who's ever taken a shower has an idea. It's the person who gets out of the shower, dries off and does something about it who makes the difference.
>
> **Nolan Bushnell, founder of Atari and Chuck E. Cheese's restaurants**

When you think of the success of Silicon Valley and its computer software companies, you probably picture all the brilliant young computer scientists who settle there. You remember Stanford's early, earthshaking contributions to computer science and engineering. You think of all the hot, innovative companies headquartered there, and the ideas that travel like pollen from one to the next.

Those are all factors in the region's success. But a lesser-known, equally powerful reason that the world looks to Silicon Valley for game-changing innovation is a new approach to product innovation called *design thinking*. And at the center of this new approach is the world's most famous product design firm, IDEO—next door to Stanford, Apple, and Google, smack in the middle of a dense cluster of world-famous technology firms.

The core of design thinking is *getting ideas out into the world as early as possible*. This is called "rapid prototyping"—taking an idea and making a simple version of it in an hour or a day. Designers surround themselves with materials that can be manipulated and shaped quickly and cheaply, like clay; cardboard; and foam core (a strong and lightweight sheet that's a bit like superthick cardboard, but easy to cut into whatever shape you need).

Tom Kelley, the general manager of IDEO, describes creatives as people "who make ideas tangible—dashing off sketches, cobbling together creations from duct tape and foam core, shooting quick videos to give personality and shape to a new concept." Dennis Boyle, a veteran lead designer at IDEO, creates several models and prototypes every week, and shares them all with clients. As Kelley writes,

> To do is to be.
>
> *Jean-Jacques Rousseau*

> There's always something that wasn't clear at the last meeting that you can clarify by showing how you might implement a hinge or mount a display or control a specific mechanism. Prototyping is a way of making progress when the challenges seem insurmountable.

Here's an example of how IDEO's process works. Designer Sean Corcorran was leading a team that was designing a new office chair. At one point, they were stumped: they couldn't figure out the lever that would adjust the chair's height. They needed the lever to tilt along with the chair, but how could they manage that? To work through the impasse, they started making things. In just a couple of hours, they built a simple lever and a way for it to connect to the release mechanism. From the way the prototype fit in Sean's hand, he knew the design would work. Design thinking is *thinking made visible*, thinking through making.

The success of IDEO is living proof that the act of making is what drives constant creativity. When you make something real—whether you're modeling a lever in 3-D or acting out a stage play or sewing an original dress design in muslin to see if it works—the act of making often leads you to new ideas. That's because the real world

To be is to do.

Jean-Paul Sartre

holds surprises. We can't anticipate its zigs and zags. When IDEO was designing a new video game steering wheel for Logitech, its designers wanted to build a prototype out of black rubber. Alas, they were out of black rubber, so they ended up using some red rubber they had in the shop. Turned out Logitech loved the color, and the game company released a trademark line of red steering wheels.

EVAPORATE

THEY

REALITY

INTO

MASSAGED

ARE

IDEAS

UNLESS

Kids understand this step; they love to make things. At a young age, they start with wooden blocks and Tinkertoys, and then they graduate to cardboard and tape and markers. I used to sketch out board games. I'd use graph paper and invent games with X's and O's just to pass the time. When I was a teenager, I used my dad's power tools to make the games I'd sketched, cutting dowel rods apart and drilling holes in wood blocks.

A simple game I made as a teenager.

Other teenagers learn how to wire electronics, sculpt the human form, build structures out of spare scraps of wood, or repair engines. Quite a lot of exceptional creators were makers as children. Steven Chu, winner of the 1997 Nobel Prize in Physics, says in his Nobel autobiography:

> In the summer after kindergarten, a friend introduced me to the joys of building plastic model airplanes and warships. By the fourth grade, I graduated to an Erector set and spent many happy hours constructing devices of unknown purpose where the main design criterion was to maximize the number of moving parts and overall size... The years of experience building things taught me skills that were directly applicable [to physics].

Thinkering (noun). Thinking while tinkering.

At the San Francisco Exploratorium, the world's most famous science center, one of the most popular exhibits is called the Tinkering Workshop. The museum's interpreters cover a large table with scraps of cardboard, rolls of tape, and wooden sticks, and they provide a few tips about how to make mechanical devices. The kids take it from there.

The word "thinkering" was coined by writer Michael Ondaatje in his novel *The English Patient*. It describes a powerful tool for creativity: when we tinker with our hands, we're more likely to have new ideas. We usually assume that creativity starts with a mental idea, and that once it's completely thought out, we start to make it. But psychologists have recently shown that that's backward, just as Ondaatje observed. New studies show that our innermost thoughts are built on bodily action, not the other way around.

Vera John-Steiner, a psychologist at the University of New Mexico, interviewed over seventy exceptional creators—from composer Aaron Copland to author Anaïs Nin—and studied their diaries and notebooks.

> Successful creators engage in an ongoing dialogue with their work. They put what's in their head on paper long before it's fully formed, and they watch and listen to what they've recorded, zigging and zagging until the right idea emerges.

Amazingly, John-Steiner was the first psychologist to imagine that these notebooks could provide a window into the daily work habits of their creators. She also studied the notebooks of another fifty historical creators, such as Diego Riviera, Leo Tolstoy, and Marie Curie. She started with this question: "What nourishes sustained productivity in the lives of creative individuals?" She had the same assumption most of us have: that ideas come first, and the real work follows. She was so certain of this that she initially planned to call her book *The Leap*, because she thought she'd be writing about that legendary big flash of insight that comes only to geniuses.

She found just the opposite. Creativity started with the notebooks' sketches and jottings, and only later resulted in a pure, powerful idea. The one characteristic that all of these creatives shared—whether they were painters, actors, or scientists—was how often they put their early thoughts and inklings out into the world, in sketches, dashed-off phrases and observations, bits of dialogue, and quick prototypes. Instead of arriving in one giant leap, great creations emerged by zigs and zags as their creators engaged over and over again with these externalized images. Here are just a few examples:

- Albert Einstein always said he thought in pictures: "Words do. not play any role in my thought; instead, I think in signs and images which I can copy and combine."
- English writer Jessica Mitford engaged in a constant dialogue with her unfolding drafts: "The first thing to do is read over what you have done the day before and rewrite it. And then that gives you a lead into the next thing to do."
- The painter Ben Shahn described creativity as "the long artistic tug-of-war between idea and image."
- Poet May Sarton wrote, "The poem teaches us something while we make it; there is nothing dull about revision."

Successful creators engage in an ongoing dialogue with their work. They put what's in their head on paper long before it's fully formed, and they watch and listen to what they've recorded, zigging and zagging until the right idea emerges. Making doesn't come at the end of the process; it's embedded throughout, always alternating with the other seven steps. When you work this way, you're constantly making, and each time you make something, you then choose whether it's worth pursuing or not. Making helps you refine your idea, and it often leads to new questions, new ideas, and new fusions of ideas.

The Practices

When you're a master maker, you instinctively, impulsively externalize your idea. You put it into words and explain it to someone else. You shape it into an object, you build it, you rotate it and touch it. You draw a floor plan for the country house in your murder mystery. You make a tiny clay model that could wind up as a giant metal sculpture. You paint swaths of different colors on a wall, tack up wallpaper samples, and set down squares of carpet to find a color scheme for the interior you're designing.

As you make your idea, it takes on a life of its own. You can modify it and experiment with it. You explore how it works and survives. You learn where to invest future efforts, and what follow-on ideas are needed to make your original idea even better.

Making involves mastering five practices: Draw It, See It, Build It, Make It Concrete, and Reflect on It.

The First Practice of Making: Draw It

These techniques help you to get your ideas onto the page. If you're just learning to be a creative maker, this practice is the easiest way to begin. No artistic ability required, I promise!

 Draw a Picture

Pablo Picasso filled up eight notebooks just doing preliminary sketches for his revolutionary Cubist painting *Les Demoiselles d'Avignon*. But you don't have to be a brilliant artist to tap into the power of drawing. Anyone can doodle. Remember, the only person who needs to know what you've sketched is you. So nurture your inner doodler—at boring meetings, during tedious phone calls, while your great aunt Lucinda catches you up on her cats' ailments . . .

What about abstract problems, like your relationship with your teenage daughter, or the impossible workload you're facing? Nothing is too abstract to draw. In fact, the most abstract problems are the ones that benefit the most from

> In the brush doing what it's doing, it will stumble on what one couldn't do by oneself.
>
> *Robert Motherwell, American painter*

visualization. Even if your problem is highly conceptual, translate it into an image and draw a picture of it. Your daughter won't listen? Draw her with her hands over her ears, and arrows coming at her from you, her teachers, and her coach. You're studying Søren Kierkegaard's "leap of faith" in philosophy class? Draw two cliffs with a chasm between them, then sketch in a tiny stick figure hesitating at the edge of one cliff, foot outstretched.

It can help to cartoonify your idea, using bold, exaggerated shapes, or to iconize it with simple symbols, as if you were playing "Pictionary" and drawing a simple picture to get your teammate to guess what your idea is. Try using icons in the following exercise, and pick a practical, "process" sort of problem, such as "How can we reduce waiting times in the emergency room?"

First, you'll need a stack of index cards. Begin by breaking the problem down into a set of variables or attributes (you might want to refer back to the Break It Down technique in Chapter One). Try for at least five, and no more than ten. Here are variables I came up with for the emergency room problem:

- Where people sit while they wait
- How people arrive
- What sorts of illnesses or injuries they have
- What types of staff and services are available to treat them
- How patients will pay for services
- Who else is waiting with them

Now, take each of the attributes and create an icon that represents it—in the emergency room example, maybe a chair, an ambulance, a heart with a lightning bolt through it for cardiac arrest . . . you get the idea. Use a separate index card for each icon.

Once you're finished with your cards, lay them all out on a table. Spend some time looking at them and moving them around to make different configurations. Try rearranging them and see which combinations pop out and make the most sense. Look for unexpected connections. Maybe the person accompanying the patient is the person who will be paying, so that person can do the checking in

For some people, adding color into the mix enhances creativity. Remember that great sixty-four-color crayon box with the built-in sharpener? Buy yourself one now, or get a jumbo set of felt-tip markers or fine-point Sharpies. Personally, I prefer fat crayons in a short glass on my desk, because they remind me of my childhood, and that puts me in the mind-set of lighthearted, freethinking play.

while the patient goes straight to the waiting nurses. (By the way, don't just throw out the cards! Save them in a special place, because you'll be able to use some of them later with a completely unrelated problem. Icons are abstract by nature, and can be interpreted in many different ways.)

Collaborate

Getting ideas down on paper can do wonders for group creativity. Here's a technique that works beautifully to generate a flow of ideas once the problem has been identified and defined. For visual, design, and engineering problems, bring together a group of four or five designers. Ask each designer to sketch a possible solution to the problem. They should all work independently (and without talking) for five minutes. Then, have each person pass his or her sketch to the next person. Take five more minutes, encouraging each designer to add to, modify, or delete portions of his or her colleague's design. Keep passing the sketches until each person has had a chance to work on every design. Here's an example done by a group of four designers:

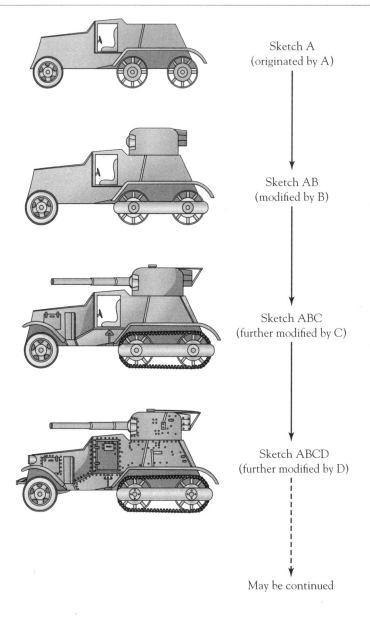

Sketch A
(originated by A)

Sketch AB
(modified by B)

Sketch ABC
(further modified by C)

Sketch ABCD
(further modified by D)

May be continued

The real benefit of this technique comes when a designer misinterprets the original intention of an element in a colleague's sketch, because that leads the designers to zig zag down an unexpected path, resulting in more surprising and more original solutions. That's why it's important that no one talks!

You can use a similar technique if you're trying to come up with a mission statement or a slogan or a headline or a product name. Have each person come up with five possibilities and then start passing the ideas around and let people edit, add to, and play off of each other's ideas.

The Second Practice of Making: See It

These techniques help you use images from the world around you to make your ideas.

 Take Photos

Carry a small digital camera around with you (or just use your cell phone's camera). Make a point of taking at least ten photos every day for a week. Pick a theme for each day first thing in the morning, either a visual characteristic or something more abstract:

- Circles
- People standing (or waiting for a bus, or queued for tickets, or smoking outside their office . . .)
- People laughing
- People using their smartphone
- Improvised fixes for problems—like eyeglasses held together by a paper clip, or an old car's bumper held in place with a rope
- Images that suggest loneliness (or excitement, or chaos . . .)

Save all of your photos in a special folder on your computer to make it easy to look through them later. Give the folder a name that will remind you of the theme. At the end

> The hardest thing to see is what is in front of your eyes.
>
> *Johann Wolfgang von Goethe*

of the day, study the photos and look for subtexts and patterns and shared characteristics. At the end of the week, spend a few minutes looking through all seven days of photos, hunting for connections across the different days' themes.

Photos aren't the only way to see what you're doing. When I was designing *Neon*, my attempt at a 1980s-style New Wave video game, I knew what aesthetic we'd want: bright, primary colors; lots of triangles; and neon art. During the year I was working on the game, I also designed a neon wall sculpture for my apartment: I got a piece of plexiglass, cut it into a triangle shape, painted the back of it black, and paid a neon lighting expert to make three bars of neon in three different shades of blue. That was our visual aesthetic, and it kept us on track.

 Gather Photos

Spend some time on an Internet photo-sharing site like Flickr (or Pinterest, or Shutterfly, or Instagram). Look for pictures of physical action—pictures that have energy and movement, as opposed to still life shots or abstract art shots. Create a picture file on your computer to save the photos that interest you.

Use this library anytime you're stumped. Select one of the photos at random and then free-associate and brainstorm connections between the photo and your creative challenge.

You can do this in a group, too: print out at least ten of these photos, and ask everyone in the group to react to each image. After each person speaks, take a few minutes for the rest of the group to build on that reaction with new connections and ideas.

 Make a Collage

This technique works best when your problem is already well defined and formulated, and you need a creative solution to move forward.

Buy a stack of magazines, at least ten. Look for glossy magazines with lots of pictures, and get a variety of types—sports, lifestyle, business. Spread them out on a table, and look through each magazine, noticing only the photos and ads. Clip out any photo that seems connected to your problem in any way whatsoever, even if the connection is very remote. In half an hour, you should be able to clip out well over fifty separate images.

Now grab a glue stick and make a collage by fixing the images to a large piece of poster board. Arrange them so there's a logic to their positioning. Don't worry if a creative solution doesn't come to you while you're doing this; for the moment, your goal is simply to make the collage.

Once you're done, hang the collage on the wall next to your desk, someplace you (and your colleagues) will see it every day. (If everyone in the group does this, you can rotate the collages every morning so you each gaze at a new collage daily.) Whenever you take a break from work, spend a minute or so studying the collage. Let your mind wander. Chances are that you'll notice something you didn't notice before, and you may be surprised by a new perspective on your problem.

The Third Practice of Making: Build It

These techniques encourage you to make a 3-D model of your ideas.

 Try Quick and Dirty

In hockey, it's almost never a bad idea to shoot the puck at the goalie, even if you're pretty sure the goalie will block the shot. Just getting the puck near the goal can make unexpected things happen. Besides, if the puck is nowhere near the goal, you sure as heck won't get it in the net.

Speed counts. Work like designers at IDEO: build your idea in ten minutes or less. Don't get blocked by trying to make it look great. Make it cheap and fast: cut up a cereal box and tape pieces together, or get some toothpicks and clay. You can use any old box or cardboard, or you can go to your local art supply store and buy some foam core. It's not that expensive, and then you're ready to prototype just like the professionals.

Go ahead and take the shot.

 ### Construct It

Even the most abstract problems can be made into physical reality. The Lego Group now has a consulting practice, Lego Serious Play, which guides teams of executives as they work with Legos to build very abstract things, like their company's corporate culture.

Use a children's construction set to build your idea:

- Legos
- Tinkertoys
- An Erector Set
- Modeling clay
- Silly Putty
- Four different colors of Play-Doh

My own favorite is the Tinkertoys—they're colorful, they're quick and easy, and the construction ends up being surprisingly large. I also keep a Ziploc bag of about forty Lego pieces in my briefcase for those times when I have nothing to do. Build with the Lego pieces whenever you might otherwise be fidgeting, like when you're on a long conference call. Why not fidget productively?

 ### Visit a Craft Store

Your local craft store can be a source of great creativity. You should make a habit of browsing the store a couple of times each year. Your mission: come out with a bagful of stuff that you could then use to make a version of your idea.

Walk slowly through the aisles, checking out the infinite variety of wooden, Styrofoam, plastic, and metal objects that people use to make stuff. If something catches your eye, go ahead and buy it! It probably costs less than a dollar. Don't worry yet about what you'll be making when you get home. Don't plan or use a shopping list. Just let your eyes wander, and grab what intrigues you.

After one visit to a craft store, I made a construction kit for my children. I bought artist's modeling clay in three different colors. I broke each block apart, and rolled the pieces into balls that were each about half an inch in diameter. Then I bought a box of colored toothpicks, to use to link two of the small clay balls together. By the time I was finished I'd made my own version of a Tinkertoy construction kit. And I had as much fun making it as my children did playing with it!

The Fourth Practice of Making: Make It Concrete

These techniques help you transform abstract, conceptual thinking into an external, visible form. Even very abstract ideas can be made to come to life.

 Chart the Flow

For many creative challenges, the solution will be a process rather than an object. Our emergency room problem, for example, probably needs a process solution. So in this case, try this: draw a flowchart. A flowchart is a method originally developed by computer programmers to visually represent what a computer program will do at each step. It shows decision points where the program's path will change, depending on your answer to particular questions.

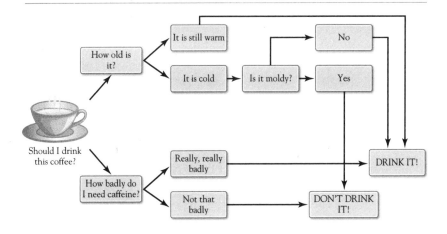

Start with your desired end state on the right-hand side of the paper and your current state on the left-hand side. Fill in the space in between with a flowchart that could potentially lead to a solution. The more detail, and the more decision points, the better. It especially helps if many of those decision points have branching possible futures; you can then figure out a way to make all of them lead to the solution.

 Map the Journey

Here's a second technique that works particularly well for process problems—using anything that happens over time, whether you're getting through the emergency room or Disney World or developing a new customer experience at a giant retail store. For creative challenges like these, you need a way to visualize the events as they unfold. Unless you're focusing on a mental process, you'll be talking about an experience that moves through space as well as time. Sketch it as a journey. Get inspired by geography, by the topography of the places you know well. Think in metaphors: draw mountains for blocks and challenges; draw rivers for movement and transition. Maybe even use volcanoes and caves for dangers and pitfalls. The key is to ask yourself, "How does my customer cross this terrain?

What's that experience like? How can I design the best possible journey?"

 Sing It

Choose a simple, common melody and make up lyrics that describe your idea. Use a song everyone knows: "Jingle Bells," "Happy Birthday to You," or "Turkey in the Straw."

Or, if you prefer to focus on the rhythm of the words rather than the melody, create a rap song.

Or, write a thirty-second advertising jingle for your idea—make it catchy and to the point.

 Act It Out

If your creative challenge involves people and relationships, why not act out possible creative solutions? Invite a trusted friend or colleague to do a short role-play with you. Acting out solutions can make all sorts of relationship ideas concrete:

The U.S. military often acts out potential situations using *simulations*—they engage hundreds or thousands of soldiers and officers and have them enact a possible solution to a potential real-world problem.

- *Service encounters*: selling a product, answering a customer complaint phone call, giving advice to a shopper
- *Personal relationships*: dealing with a rebellious teenager, discussing a long-standing problem with a spouse
- *Workplace issues*: managing a difficult employee or colleague, asking your boss for time off

The Fifth Practice of Making: Reflect on It

Making helps you reflect on your own unfolding ideas. When I played keyboard in an early-1980s New Wave band, our drummer had a recording studio in his basement. We played all original songs (and told ourselves we sounded like the Talking Heads). Being in that recording studio changed the way I thought about music. We were making it incrementally, step-by-step. Somebody would come up with words and a harmonic structure, the drummer would find a rhythmic pattern that worked, the bass player and I would add layers to the music, and we'd improvise until it all fit together. Then, to put it down on tape, we'd record one instrument at a time, each on its own track—starting with the drums; then the bass, guitar, and keyboards; and then vocals at the very end. We went through session after session, polishing and changing the various tracks, zigging and zagging until we could hear it all working.

These three techniques help you layer, refine, and build your ideas, so they're always getting better.

 Be a Pack Rat

If you keep at the first four practices, you'll end up with a lot of sketches, models, and collages. They'll take up a lot of room, but keep them around—and warn your spouse not to throw them away in a burst of spring-cleaning.

You'll have Lego models and Tinkertoy structures. Don't pull apart the pieces to reuse them; instead, go buy some more. It won't be long before you have a lot of these constructions lying around. There will be clutter! If you can't stand having them underfoot, keep a bookshelf or a separate table to display them. *Don't* put them out of sight in a closet; you need to see them every day, even if it's just out of the corner of your eye while you're working on something else. (Instead, take the books that used to be on your bookshelf and put *them* in the closet—you'll still be able to access them, but you don't need to *see* them every day.) In supercreative companies, you see these structures and images everywhere—Tinkertoy towers on the carpet, sketches and collages on the wall.

Figure Out Origins

Every week or two, take ten or fifteen minutes to look through what you've made. Reflect on the process that led you through this sequence of artifacts. How did your ideas evolve? How do these artifacts trace a path to your current thinking?

You may decide you'd be better off if you returned to an earlier stage step, but reformulated and extended with your latest thinking, a new perspective that you didn't have back when you first made that artifact.

 Show and Tell

All the research shows that making your ideas leads to greater creativity. But making has another benefit: it leads to better collaboration. That's because after you make your ideas, other people can see them. Don't hide your ideas in your office. Take them with you when you get coffee, or when you go into a conference room. Or, if you're not ready to go public, invite a friend or a trusted colleague to take a look.

Showing your ideas works better than talking about your ideas. When you make something, it always has multiple potential interpretations. Visual images spark unexpected connections and later ideas. Listen closely when your friend sees a possibility or relationship you didn't even intend.

How Do You Know When to Stop?

In a life filled with creativity, you'll make some really cool things. And pretty soon you'll make something that you're convinced is terrific. You'll get hyperfocused and obsessive, fixated on working on your brainchild. The problem is, this focus often happens way too early in the creative process, when an even better idea is still waiting to be discovered, and there are still many zigs and zags ahead. And that first terrific idea can block your mind from generating additional ideas.

The zig zag path is one of constant evolution, ever-present change.

It's a natural instinct to latch onto an exciting idea, because we all want the exhilaration of finding the right idea, and the relief of getting the problem solved. Resist that temptation. Never fall in love with what you've made. Always be ready to make it better.

In 1956 a famous French film team of cinematographer Claude Renoir and director Henri-Georges Clouzot made a movie of Picasso painting. One of his paintings took several hours to finish, so Renoir took a photo of the canvas every five minutes, and then showed the audience a quicker time-lapse version of the entire creative process. In the speeded-up version, we watch as Picasso covers the canvas with a complete painting in what seems to be a few quick minutes. Then he starts to paint over a corner of that painting—and that gives him another idea, and he starts to paint over another corner. Just minutes later, the entire painting has changed completely. He ends up painting over his work and starting from scratch at least four times!

In 1956 Picasso was already famous; if he'd stopped along the way, he could've sold each of those four or five paintings for thousands of dollars. But creativity isn't about the money. It's about getting to the best solution. That's what makes great artists great—they don't fall in love with what they've made.

In a life of constant making, how do you know when you're done?

The answer is: *never*. You're never finished. The zig zag path is one of constant evolution, ever-present change. You are moving from one challenge to the next; you are moving through the eight steps that successful creators use. Our creativity romantics would say that great creativity comes from being blessed with a great idea. But ideas are easy; creativity is hard work. Remember that quotation from the artist Chuck Close?

"Inspiration is for amateurs, and the rest of us just show up and get to work."

Conclusion

The important thing is to create. Nothing else matters; creation is all.

Pablo Picasso

I've presented the eight steps in a row, as if they happen one after the other. This is a helpful way to understand the creative process, especially when you're just starting to realize your inner creative potential. But to truly master your creative ability, you need one final skill: the ability to bring together all eight steps to move you forward on the zig zag path.

Zig zag masters take all eight steps, every day, in whatever order works for them. Because the creative life weaves the steps together so tightly, it's hard for an observer to pick them apart. But look at the arrows in the figure that follows:

1. **Asking** leads you to **look** for the right things.
2. **Playing** leads you to discover new problems and to **ask** the right questions.
3. **Thinking** of new ideas often leads you to **ask** new questions.

4. **Learning** provides the raw material for **thinking**.

5. **Thinking** generates ideas that can then be **fused**.

6. **Making** your ideas leads to follow-on ideas and more **fusing**.

7. When you **make** an idea, it often leads you to **ask** your questions in a different way.

8. When you **choose** an idea, it often leads you to **look** at the world differently.

9. **Thinking** of a new idea prepares you to **make** it.

10. **Asking** the right questions can show you how to **fuse** your previous ideas together.

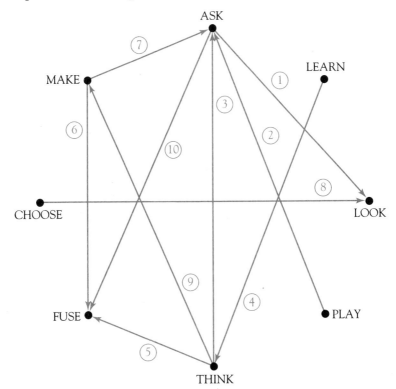

Think back through all of the stories I've told in this book; you can find examples of each of these ten arrows in one or more of those stories. And I could have added a lot more arrows; for example, I intentionally left out most of the linear arrows that go straight through the eight steps in order, but sometimes that's the way it happens. You can probably think of an example of an arrow that doesn't appear here; try to imagine how looking might lead to making, or how playing might lead to choosing.

When you're just begin-ning to practice the steps, you may need to focus on one at a time. Emphasizing one step a day is a fine way to train yourself in the zig zag way. But when you become a zig zag master, you'll shift effortlessly among the eight steps, within the same day or even within the same hour. They aren't stages in a linear process of creativity. You could take the steps in order for the rest of your life, solving one problem after another. But the process is more effective—and you'll be more creative—if you can apply them instinctively, and sometimes simultaneously.

> Here's an idea: randomly assign yourself one step to focus on each day. You can do this by rolling an eight-sided die; these are easy to find at any game store.

Learn to Choose the Right Step

Once you break creativity into these eight universal steps, it becomes much easier to know what to do when you're stumped.

When to Focus on Asking

Asking the right question might be the most important of all eight steps. After all, the zig zag path starts with a creative challenge, a problem, or an identified need. This first step gets the ball rolling.

But it would be a mistake to set your question rigidly and then move on down the path, never worrying again about the question. Remember from Chapter One that exceptional creators ask questions no one has thought of before. Your goal is to become a *problem finder*, not just a problem solver. The three practices of asking--Find the Question, Search the Space, and Transform the Problem—help you find the kinds of questions that are more likely to lead to successful creativity. With practice, you'll learn how to move beyond asking familiar and obvious questions, and start asking questions no one has considered previously.

Along the way, new questions will emerge unexpectedly—that's what leads to new zigs and zags. So don't ignore new questions; consider them carefully. In some cases, the new question will be better than the question you started out with, and you'll zig down a new path. In other cases, the new question is really a completely new project; put it aside for now, but make sure to record it in your notebook of really good questions and problems. After a few months of following these practices, you'll have found so many great problems to work on, you'll be unlikely to run out of interesting new projects.

- Problems that are best addressed with the practices of asking often first appear to be problems in another step. When you're stumped and can't come up with any ideas, when you have writer's block, when you're in a rut, your natural tendency is to try to think of a solution. But in many instances the problem is that you're trying to answer the wrong question. So when you're blocked and not moving forward, always spend some time asking yourself new questions.
- When you're trying to choose from among your ideas and none of them seems quite right, why not try revisiting your question?
- When you're making your idea—putting it out into the world—and it's just not coming out the way you anticipated, check again to see if you can't rephrase your question.

In the zigs and zags of the creative process, there will be many moments when you're not really sure where you're going or what the problem is. Accept that uncertainty, embrace its ambiguity and openness, and focus on asking.

When to Focus on Learning

Like asking, learning tends to be more prominent at the beginning of your creative journey. Every zig and zag is enhanced when you've learned everything about what has come before, what other people have tried, and what has and has not worked.

For example, it's almost impossible to ask good questions if you haven't learned what has come before. In almost any field, the experts are distinguished by their ability to ask the really good, important questions. Are you confident you've learned everything relevant to your problem? If not, you probably need to focus on the four practices of learning—Practice Deliberately, Master Your Domain, Learn Forever, and Balance Specialty with Generality.

Here's a clear signal that you need to spend time on learning: you find yourself asking questions that have already been answered. If this happens more than once, stop—you're wasting time going down these well-worn paths. Step back, and focus on learning.

Another signal that you need more learning is that it's pretty easy to answer your question. That sounds wonderful, right? But what usually happens when it's too easy is that the answer turns out to be unimportant.

What if you've done just the opposite—what if you've come up with a question that seems impossibly, ridiculously hard? Wouldn't that be the time to learn more about it? Paradoxically, the answer is probably no. When you've discovered a great question, you're better off investing your energy in the other steps, particularly look and think.

When to Focus on Looking

Active, open looking is often the source of a zig or zag down a new path. If you're skilled at looking, you'll find yourself switching direction often, as you stumble on surprising new information and as new perspectives on your problem are revealed.

Remember in Chapter Three when we learned about failure indices? Those are memory traces—sort of like bookmarks—left in your mind when you've been working on a problem and you're stumped, or you've tried a solution and it didn't work. When your mind is filled with these failure indices, you'll surprise yourself by seeing solutions to those stored problems when you least expect it.

If this isn't happening to you, it could be for two different reasons. The first possibility is that your daily creative practices aren't leaving failure indices in your mind. That could happen if you're not working on really hard, challenging problems. If you're never failing, you're never storing failure indices, and that probably means you're playing it too safe. It feels good to walk down a straight path to success, to be sure, but if you're not zigging and zagging, then you're not seeing the world actively and creatively. The second possibility is that you may not be exposing yourself to enough new stimuli. The three practices of looking—Use Fresh Eyes, Grab New Sights and Cool Sounds, and Render It Visible—are designed to teach you how to see the world the way that the most exceptional creators do.

If you're stumped, if you're stuck in a rut, if your mind keeps taking you down the same well-worn path over and over, then you need some surprising new information. Get yourself out into the world and look at it with creative eyes.

When to Focus on Playing

Are you working all the time? Do you stay late at the office? Do you find yourself working on the weekends? Did you skip your annual vacation last year? If this sounds like you, you may need to take a break, and find some time to play.

The discipline of playing helps you create space in your schedule, and that space gives your unconscious mind an opportunity to suggest ideas and solutions. Every study of exceptional creativity has found that famous creators work very hard. And yet, they also take time off—they take frequent breaks throughout the day, as well as the occasional weekend getaway and annual vacation.

In many workplaces, if you take time off, your coworkers will think you're lazy and you're not getting your job done. You're supposed to be at your desk, being productive. The benefits of playing are elusive, even a bit counterintuitive. It seems odd that you could move forward when you're not doing anything.

If you're lucky enough to have a job that you love, you get satisfaction from hard work. This can make it hard to stop working and take a break. That's why I've shared with you the research showing that creativity benefits from playing. I hope that after learning about this research you can convince yourself that you need some time to play—that you're not just wasting time.

The good news is that there are ways to enhance the value of your time off. The four practices of playing—Visualize, Relax, Find the Right Box, and Be a Beginner—contain techniques that will maximize the creative potential of your play time. Absolutely, you need to work hard to attain high levels of creativity. But, in addition, you need to find time to play.

When to Focus on Thinking

If you've turned to this fifth step in hopes of finding a great idea, you probably shouldn't be here. I could rephrase this in the style of a Zen koan:

He who is looking for a great idea will never find it.

In the Introduction, I warned you about the second creativity mistake: hoping there's one great idea out there. When people first think about creativity, they associate it with having great ideas. Many books about creativity focus on the legendary moment of insight, with titles like *Aha!* and *Spark* and even *How to Get Ideas*. Yes, of course, thinking of good ideas is a key step along the creative path. But resist your natural instinct to solve problems by jumping to this step.

When you need ideas, most of the time you're better off practicing another step instead. If you have writer's block and ideas aren't flowing, focus on the steps learn, make, and play first—and only then on think. That's because the best ideas tend to emerge after you've learned all of the relevant information, while you're playing or making.

So when *is* it appropriate to focus on thinking?

After reading the Zen koan I just made up, my advice here might sound contradictory: you should be thinking all the time. But after all, apparent contradictions are at the heart of Zen! In the creative life, thinking is embedded in everyday work habits. You use the three practices of thinking—Ideate, Transform, and Schedule—to generate a flurry of small ideas every day. You'll know you're on the wrong track if you find yourself desperately in need of a solution on Friday afternoon at 3 p.m., and yet you didn't have any ideas the whole week before that.

Start with the third practice, Schedule, and create some time every day to generate ideas. During that time, use the first two practices to generate long lists of surprising new ideas. Then your creative life will be filled with lots of small ideas, and these small ideas will weave together and build up to greatness.

When to Focus on Fusing

The three practices of thinking are designed to guarantee you a steady stream of new ideas, every day. The central message of this book is that every successful, life-changing creation comes at the end of a zig zag path, with many small ideas along the way. The three practices of fusing help you combine those small ideas into the final creative solution. Unlike with thinking, you don't necessarily need to fuse every day. It's more beneficial to fuse every week or every month.

There are several ways to know that you're ready to use the three practices of fusing—Force-Fuse, Make Analogies, and Do a People Mash-Up.

If you have lots of ideas but they're all pretty predictable, try fusing to explore some unlikely combinations. Remember, from Chapter Six, the fascinating psychological finding that more distant combinations result in more surprising and original ideas? Use fusing to get you there.

If you're far along in your project—if you've been at it for several months or years—then you should be spending progressively more time on fusing. That's because you'll have a large pool of ideas (and, yes, dead ends and failures as well), resulting in more raw material suitable for fusing. Toward the end of a project, most of your creative solutions will result from fusing past material.

You'll fuse much more naturally if you're working on multiple projects at the same time. In Chapter Six, we learned about Mihaly Csikszentmihalyi's study of ninety-six famous, exceptional creators—and found that they all worked on more than one project at a time. So if you, too, are working on multiple projects, you should probably visit this step more frequently—because you'll have so many more opportunities for surprising new connections.

When to Focus on Choosing

Perhaps more than any other of the eight steps, choose is closely associated with the end point of creativity. In pretty much all of the linear versions of the creative process, "generating ideas" is followed by "evaluating and selecting ideas."

But now you know the reality: creativity is not a linear process, with one great idea selected after a morning brainstorming session. Creativity is a zig zag path, with lots of small ideas emerging daily. And every day, you need to choose which ones to pursue.

When you're using the practices of thinking to generate lots of ideas, most of those ideas won't be chosen. And of the ideas you select to pursue, most of them will turn out to be dead ends. The good news is that working on a failed idea is what zigs and zags you to the next *better* idea.

There are a few signs indicating that you're ready to draw on the four practices of choosing—Know What You're Looking For; Host an Idea Competition; Look Past the Good; and Edit, Revise, Improve.

One sign is that you aren't failing very often. If your path from problem to solution moves in a straight line, you're probably not being very creative. Seek out the zig zag and embrace it!

The ever-repeating cycle of reviewing and improving is what drives the zig zag process forward.

A second sign is that your failures don't add up to anything. Yes, exceptional creators fail a lot, but they benefit from those failures because each one drives the process forward. If you look back and your failures each tend to be a depressing waste of time, then try these four practices.

A third sign is that your ideas are not evolving. Even the best ideas can always be made better. When you're a master at choosing, you instinctively look for ways to modify and improve each idea. The ever-repeating cycle of reviewing and improving is what drives the zig zag process forward.

When to Focus on Making

Last but *definitely* not least! The eighth step, make, is in some ways the most important. More than with any other step, making should be happening every day. Your work area should be filled with visible evidence of your creative process: your ideas (and your failures!) should be posted on the walls, the shelves, the bulletin board, and the whiteboard. Sticky notes might be lined up along the edges of your computer screen. If that doesn't sound like you, then you may need to focus on making.

Frankly, that's what I need to do. I'm the sort of person who tends to keep everything inside, an "in-the-head" kind of person. If you're like me, you need to work on the five practices of making—Draw It, See It, Build It, Make It Concrete, and Reflect on It.

In Chapter Eight, we learned of Vera John-Steiner's study of seventy successful creators. Their daily practice involved constantly externalizing their ideas, in notebooks and jottings, and then engaging in an ongoing dialogue with their work. Making didn't come at the end of the process; it was embedded throughout, and was always alternating with the other seven steps.

> In creative work, a single product is just a temporary resting place in the continuous and demanding process.
>
> *Vera John-Steiner*

- If you're having trouble figuring out exactly what the problem is and how to formulate it, try using techniques from these five practices. Making often leads to asking the right question.
- If you're having trouble coming up with good ideas, try one of these techniques. Making often leads to thinking of surprising new ideas.
- If you're having trouble deciding which of your many ideas to pursue, try one of these techniques. Making often makes it crystal clear which idea is most promising, helping you choose the best way to move forward.

And of course, at the end of the day, the only ideas that change the world are ideas that make it out into the world. You owe it to your ideas, you owe it to yourself, you owe it to the world, to translate your creativity into reality.

Discover Your Own Style

In the creative life, you're always balancing many paradoxes.

How do I balance collaboration with solitary concentration?

Your goal should be to develop a sixth sense that tells you when you need to seek out conversation and stimulus and feedback. Everyone has a unique creative rhythm that works best—just the right balance of focused work time, conversation and collaboration, playtime, and solitary relaxation. Most creators prefer to do focused work in the morning, while their mind is clear, and use the afternoon for incubation; others work late into the night, and their incubation is a long, leisurely soak in the tub the next morning.

How do I balance creative time with all of the day-to-day work I need to get done?

Don't worry about having ideas; when you follow the eight steps, the ideas will come to you.

Have you ever heard the saying "Pay yourself first"? Retirement planners use it to urge us to put away a little money in savings before we spend it all on other purposes—because that way, we're paying our future selves for a happy retirement. Exceptional creators make sure to use their best, peak time each day for their own creative activities. They're selfish about their personal energy. But for most people, the peak period is no more than about three hours—so there's a lot of time left over to take care of noncreative business.

Jealously guard your peak time. Keep it for yourself. Don't allow phone calls or e-mails or meetings to intrude. And during that time, stay disciplined. Keep yourself focused and working on the task. Don't go get coffee or take a walk; you'll be doing that later, after your work time is over.

How do I know when it's time to move forward?

For zig zag masters, the eight steps overlap and link together. These creators zig and zag fearlessly and intuitively from one step to another. But at the beginning, you may find it helpful to focus on one step at a time. And then, how do you know how long to stay with one step before moving on to another?

Like all good questions, this one has no easy answer. Sometimes you only need to work on one step for five minutes; at other times, you might need two or three days. When you become a zig zag master, you'll develop a second sense for when to switch steps; you'll just know. For now, pay attention to your mood. Are you getting bored or restless, losing focus, thinking ahead? Move on. Do you still feel a little hesitant and uncertain? Stay put.

The creative person: a dangerous bread

The bottom line is, you need to be extremely self-aware. Get familiar with your own creative process by constantly listening to yourself, constantly reflecting on exactly what you're doing at a given moment. Is it working? If not, what might you do instead? Why not use the make techniques and externalize a visual image of your own creative process? Exceptional creators are highly self-aware and reflective about their own creative processes because they must guard them so religiously from the world's interruptions.

Reading this book is a great way to start.

Always Onward!

A year from now, you may wish you had started today.

Karen Lamb

At the beginning of this book, I asked you to write down a couple of specific problems you wanted to solve. I'm guessing that by now, you're a lot closer to creative solutions. But now that you're engaging daily in the eight steps, new challenges will emerge, new questions you may never have noticed before. New solutions, too. This is partly because you're paying attention. But it's also because your emotional resistance is gone. When you've mastered creativity, it's no longer scary to tackle a challenge.

You're no longer afraid of the unpredictability and the uncertainty of the zig zag path. It's fun.

This book describes a daily practice, a new way of living. When you master its eight steps, creativity comes naturally to you. It seems effortless. You stop worrying about "coming up with" ideas; you know they'll come when you need them. And as I think you can tell by now, that steady flow of creativity has the potential to make your life more meaningful, more deeply fulfilling. You can accomplish what you set out to do, and you can solve many of the annoying problems that pop up along the way.

Engaging in the eight steps lets you express and better understand the thoughts and feelings, memories and experiences, affinities and desires that accumulate deep inside you. It also connects you with the larger world, rooting you firmly in both nature and society, because you're observing your surroundings so closely. And, oddly enough, it improves your relationships—a delightful benefit I hadn't expected. You're paying attention, and you're solving problems in creative ways that really work, instead of slapping on some self-help book's simplistic formula.

If you learn only one thing from this book, I hope it's this:

Creativity is not a moment in time; it's a way of life. Live the creative life. Don't worry about having ideas; when you follow the eight steps, the ideas will come to you. And the more ideas you have, the more likely you are to come upon one that's brilliant. So brilliant, it will look, to everybody else, like it came in a flash. With a leap of insight. By magic.

You'll know better.

Appendix A
Outline of All of the Steps, Practices, and Techniques

Ask
The First Practice of Asking: Find the Question

Try Ten Questions
Find the Bug
Reinterpret
Rise to the Occasion

The Second Practice of Asking: Search the Space

Break It Down
Draw a Fishbone
Map Your Idea
Challenge Your Assumptions

The Third Practice of Asking: Transform the Problem

Reverse
Go Back from the Future (BFF)
Pick the Worst Idea
Stretch and Squeeze

Learn

The First Practice of Learning: Practice Deliberately

Challenge Yourself

Focus on Specific Tasks

Reflect

The Second Practice of Learning: Master Your Domain

Get Schooled

Go for Deeper Understanding

Apply What You Know to New Situations

The Third Practice of Learning: Learn Forever

Seek Knowledge Relentlessly

Customize Knowledge

Read a Book

Stay Current

Recruit a Mentor

The Fourth Practice of Learning: Balance Specialty with Generality

Be T-Shaped

Branch Out

Be a Dilettante

Pair Up with an Expert

Look

The First Practice of Looking: Use Fresh Eyes

Become More Aware

Make Your Own Luck

Look for New Patterns

Cultivate Your Senses

Practice Ethnography

Look for Serendipity

Spot the Spandrels

Switch Perspectives

The Second Practice of Looking: Grab New Sights and Cool Sounds

Start Tripping

Relax and Listen

Play with Children's Toys

Shape Your Day

Remember to Look at *Bad* Examples

Flip Through Strange Magazines

Absorb New Media

Go Walkabout

Travel

The Third Practice of Looking: Render It Visible

Keep an Idea Log

Start an Idea Box

Set a Google Alert

Create a Personal Hall of Fame

Appoint a Personal Board of Directors

Play

The First Practice of Playing: Visualize

Imagine Parallel Worlds

Come Up with Fantastic Explanations

Envision What's Below

Follow the Long Arrow

Explore the Future

Visualize Your Space

The Second Practice of Playing: Relax

Incubate

Leave Something Undone

Still Your Mind

Listen

The Third Practice of Playing: Find the Right Box

Be Specific

Draw the Right Box

Create a New Box

Use Every Box

The Fourth Practice of Playing: Be a Beginner

Do Something for the First Time
Start a New Hobby
Plan on Fun

Think

The First Practice of Thinking: Ideate

Think Different
Try Toppling

The Second Practice of Thinking: Transform

SCAMPER
List Attributes
Reverse Again

The Third Practice of Thinking: Schedule

Set an Idea Time
Set an Idea Quota

Fuse

The First Practice of Fusing: Force-Fuse

Make Remote Associations
Combine Concepts
Cook on All Burners

The Second Practice of Fusing: Make Analogies

Use Direct Analogy

Mimic Nature

Use Personal Analogy

The Third Practice of Fusing: Do a People Mash-Up

Talk to Someone Different

Crash a Meeting

Work in the Intersection

Choose

The First Practice of Choosing: Know What You're Looking For

Train Your Intuition

Color Your Choices

Go for Simple, Elegant, Robust

Check Your Ideas

Define Greatness

The Second Practice of Choosing: Host an Idea Competition

Look for Differences

Map the Grid

Draw an Affinity Diagram

The Third Practice of Choosing: Look Past the Good

Consider Pros and Cons

Find the Worst-Case Scenario

The Fourth Practice of Choosing: Edit, Revise, Improve

Identify Three Benefits

Fix the Fatal Flaw

Be the Devil's Advocate

Reformulate, Reuse, Reperceive

Make

The First Practice of Making: Draw It

Draw a Picture

Collaborate

The Second Practice of Making: See It

Take Photos

Gather Photos

Make a Collage

The Third Practice of Making: Build It

Try Quick and Dirty

Construct It

Visit a Craft Store

The Fourth Practice of Making: Make It Concrete

Chart the Flow

Map the Journey

Sing It

Act It Out

The Fifth Practice of Making: Reflect on It

Be a Pack Rat

Figure Out Origins

Show and Tell

Appendix B
The Research Behind the Eight Steps

Psychologists have been studying the creative process for decades, and they've often observed that creativity tends to occur in a sequence of stages. The simplest model of the creative process, sometimes called the *balloon*, has two stages—an expanding stage of *divergent thinking* in which many possibilities are generated, followed by *convergent thinking* as you converge on the one best idea. The balloon is useful as shorthand, but most theories of the creative process have elaborated on the simple balloon model to propose four or more stages, giving us a deeper understanding of the mental activities in which people engage when they're creating. *Zig Zag* is organized around an integrated framework that captures the key stages of all of the various models that psychologists have proposed. In the table that follows, I show how the eight steps align with a range of psychological models of the creative process.

The material in Appendix B is excerpted, with modification, from the fifth, sixth, and seventh chapters of Sawyer (2012). If you are interested in diving into the research in more detail, you can read about scientific studies pertaining to each of the eight steps in those chapters.

	Wallas (1926)	Creative Problem Solving (Isaksen, Dorval, & Treffinger, 2000)	IDEAL cycle (Bransford & Stein, 1993)	Sternberg (2006)	Possibility Thinking (Burnard, Craft, & Grainger, 2006)	Qualifications and Curriculum Authority (QCA, 2005)	Synectics (Gordon, 1961)	Mumford's Group (Scott, Leritz, & Mumford, 2004)	IDEO (Kelley, 2001)
Ask		Framing problems	Identify problems, define goals	Redefine problems	Posing questions	Questioning and challenging		Problem finding	
Learn	Preparation	Exploring data	Learn	Know the domain			Groundwork	Information gathering	
Look			Look		Immersion	Envisaging what might be	Immersion		Observation
Play	Incubation	Constructing opportunities	Explore possible strategies	Take time off	Play	Keeping options open		Concept search	
Think	Insight	Generating ideas		Generate ideas	Being imaginative	Exploring ideas	Divergent exploration	Idea generation	Brainstorming
Fuse		Developing solutions		Cross-fertilize ideas		Making connections and seeing relationships		Conceptual combination	
Choose	Verification			Judge ideas		Reflecting critically on ideas	Selection	Idea evaluation	
Make	Elaboration	Building acceptance	Act and anticipate outcomes	Sell the idea, persevere	Self-determination		Articulation of solution, development and transformation	Implementation, planning, and action monitoring	Rapid prototyping, refining, and implementation

All of these psychologists have concluded that creativity isn't a single, unitary mental process. The consensus among them is that creativity results from many different mental processes, each associated with one or more of the eight steps.

The zig zag model is a useful way of capturing all of the cognitive processes involved in creativity. The eight steps are *domain general*; that means that the creative process in all domains, from science to technological invention to fine art painting, involves these steps.

The mental processes associated with the eight steps can overlap, or cycle repeatedly, or sometimes appear in reverse order. This is why some creativity researchers prefer to describe them as "disciplines" or "habits of mind" that are associated with highly creative individuals; some of the models cited in the table are presented this way, including those of Burnard et al. (2006) and Scott et al. (2004).

When we do intensive biographical studies that explore the origins of transformative discoveries and inventions, we see that creativity emerges over time in a complex, nonlinear fashion. Many creative products evolve over months and years, so undertaking these biographical studies involve a lot of work—poring over journals, notes, preliminary drafts, and letters. One of the most influential biographical studies was Howard Gruber's close reading of Charles Darwin's journals. Gruber's analysis of how Darwin's theory emerged over fourteen years filled a rather large book (Gruber, 1974). Most such studies require a book to tell the whole story—other examples include Seth Shulman's story (2002) of the Wright brothers, Glenn Curtiss, and the airplane, and Tom Standage's story (1998) of how the telegraph emerged from Samuel Morse's twelve-year effort. Creativity researchers are still fleshing out theories about these long-term processes: how long creative periods are sustained, and how one multiyear period is succeeded by a shift to another research question or another style of visual representation (see Feinstein, 2006; Gruber, 1988; Nakamura & Csikszentmihalyi, 2003).

Rather than coming in a single moment of insight, creativity involves a lot of hard work over an extended period of time. While doing the work, the creator experiences frequent but small mini-insights. These mini-insights are usually easy to explain in terms of the hard, conscious work that immediately preceded them. Psychologists still don't know exactly what goes on in the mind, but we do know that insights are based in previous experiences, they build on acquired knowledge and memory, and they result from combinations of existing mental material.

These psychological studies have shown that the moment of insight is overrated. It's only one small component of a complex creative process, and it's not all that mysterious. The typical creator experiences many small mini-insights every day, and these mini-insights can be traced back to the material he or she has been consciously working on. We only think we see a dramatic leap of insight because we didn't observe the many small, incremental steps that preceded it. Instead of the lightbulb, a better metaphor for an insight would be the tip of an iceberg, or the final brick in a wall. And I think the best visual image of the creative process is the zig zag (hence the name of this book). Creative activities require continual problem solving and decision making, and all decision points along the way involve a small amount of creative inspiration. When these mini-insights are viewed together in the context of the ongoing creative work, they no longer seem so mysterious. Creativity researchers today agree that "creativity takes time . . . the creative process is not generally considered to be something that occurs in an instant with a single flash of insight, even though insights may occur" (Tardif & Sternberg, 1988, p. 430).

Notes

Bransford, J. D., and Stein, B. S. (1993). *The IDEAL problem solver* (2nd ed.). New York, NY: W. H. Freeman.

Burnard, P., Craft, A., & Grainger, T. (2006). Possibility thinking. *International Journal for Early Years Education, 14*, 243–262.

Feinstein, J. S. (2006). *The nature of creative development.* Stanford, CA: Stanford Business Books.

Gordon, W.J.J. (1961). *Synectics: The development of creative capacity.* New York, NY: Harper & Row.

Gruber, H. E. (1974). *Darwin on man: A psychological study of scientific creativity.* Chicago, IL: University of Chicago Press.

Gruber, H. E. (1988). The evolving systems approach to creative work. *Creativity Research Journal, 1,* 27–51.

Isaksen, S. G., Dorval, K. B., & Treffinger, D. J. (2000). *Creative approaches to problem solving: A framework for change* (2nd ed.). Buffalo, NY: Creative Problem Solving Group.

Kelley, T. (2001). *The art of innovation: Lessons in creativity from IDEO, America's leading design firm.* New York, NY: Doubleday.

Nakamura, J., & Csikszentmihalyi, M. (2003). Creativity in later life. In R. K. Sawyer, V. John-Steiner, S. Moran, R. Sternberg, D. H. Feldman, M. Csikszentmihalyi, & J. Nakamura (Ed.), Creativity and development (pp. 186–216). New York, NY: Oxford University Press.

Qualifications and Curriculum Authority (QCA). (2005). *Creativity: Find it, promote it; Promoting pupils' creative thinking and behaviour across the curriculum at key stages 1 and 2. Practical materials for schools.* London, England: Author.

Sawyer, R. K. (2012). *Explaining creativity: The science of human innovation* (2nd edition). New York, NY: Oxford University Press.

Scott, G., Leritz, L. E., & Mumford, M. D. (2004). The effectiveness of creativity training: A quantitative review. *Creativity Research Journal, 16,* 361–388.

Shulman, S. (2002). *Unlocking the sky: Glenn Hammond Curtiss and the race to invent the airplane.* New York, NY: HarperCollins.

Standage, T. (1998). *The Victorian Internet: The remarkable story of the telegraph and the nineteenth century's on-line pioneers.* New York, NY: Walker.

Sternberg, R. J. (2006). Stalking the elusive creativity quark: Toward a comprehensive theory of creativity. In P. Locher, C. Martindale, & L. Dorfman (Eds.), *New directions in aesthetics, creativity, and the arts* (pp. 79–104). Amityville, NY: Baywood.

Tardif, T. Z., & Sternberg, R. J. (1988). What do we know about creativity? In R. J. Sternberg (Ed.), *The nature of creativity* (pp. 429–440). New York, NY: Cambridge University Press.

Wallas, G. (1926). *The art of thought.* New York, NY: Harcourt, Brace.

References

Introduction

Stephen Covey quotation. Page 68 of Covey, S. R. (1994). *Daily reflections for highly effective people*. New York, NY: Fireside.

Josh Linkner quotation. Page 145 of Linkner, J. (2011). *Disciplined dreaming: A proven system to drive breakthrough creativity*. San Francisco, CA: Jossey-Bass.

Hal Gregersen quotation. Tutton, Mark. (2009, December 1). Learn the five secrets of innovation. Retrieved from http://edition.cnn.com/2009 /BUSINESS/11/26/innovation.tips/index.html

Carl Jung quotation. Page 82 of Jung, C. (1926). *Psychological types, or the psychology of individuation*. New York, NY: Harcourt, Brace.

Martha Beck quotation. This was a "daily coach tip" she tweeted on December 30, 2010: MarthaBeck. (2010, December 30). DailyCoachTip: Don't wait for catastrophe to drive you to the depth of your being. Go there now; then you'll be ready. [Twitter post]. Retrieved from http://twitter.com/MarthaBeck/statuses/20488051998334976

Creativity doesn't come in one big idea, but rather in many small ideas. Sawyer, R. K. (2012). *Explaining creativity: The science of human innovation* (2nd ed.). New York, NY: Oxford University Press.

Virginia Woolf quotation. Page 361 of Woolf, V. (2008). *To the Lighthouse*. Ware, Hertfordshire, England: Wordsworth Editions. (Original work published 1927).

Chuck Close quotation. Page 42 of Fig, J. (2009) *Inside the painter's studio*. New York, NY: Princeton Architectural Press. Close has said much the same thing in many different contexts; he is so well known for this saying that a chapter in his biography is titled "Inspiration Is for Amateurs" (Finch, C. [2010]. *Chuck Close: Life*. Munich, Germany: Prestel Verlag).

Anne Lamott quotation. Page 21 of Lamott, A. (1994). *Bird by bird: Some instructions on writing and life.* New York, NY: Pantheon Books.

Chapter One

Peter Drucker quotation. Page 144 of Hurson, T. (2008). *Think better: An innovator's guide to productive thinking.* New York, NY: McGraw-Hill.

Starbucks story. Thompson, A. A., & Strickland, A. J. (1999). *Strategic management: Concepts and cases.* Chicago, IL: Irwin.

Clayton Christensen quotation. Page 155 of Christensen, C. (1997). *The innovator's dilemma: When new technologies cause great firms to fail.* Boston, MA: Harvard Business School Press.

Naguib Mahfouz quotation. Page 653 of St. Peter, A. (2010). *The greatest quotations of all time.* Bloomington, IN: Xlibris.

Instagram story. I drew on three sources: Systrom, K. (2010, October 8). Instagram: What is the genesis of Instagram? Retrieved from www .quora.com/Instagram/What-is-the-genesis-of-Instagram; Cutler, K.-M. (2012, April 9). From 0 to $1 billion in two years: Instagram's rose-tinted ride to glory. Retrieved from http://techcrunch.com /2012/04/09/instagram-story-facebook-acquisition/; Sengupta, S., Perlroth, N., & Wortham, J. (2012, April 13). Behind Instagram's success, networking the old way. *The New York Times.* Retrieved from www.nytimes.com/2012/04/14/technology/instagram-founders -were-helped-by-bay-area-connections.html

Scholars who argue creativity is just problem solving. Here is a sampling: Flavell, J. H., & Draguns, J. (1957). A microgenetic approach to perception and thought. *Psychological Bulletin, 54,* 197–217; Pages 312–331 of Guilford, J. P. (1967). *The nature of human intelligence.* New York, NY: McGraw-Hill; Kaufmann, G. (1988). Problem solving and creativity. In K. Grønhaug & G. Kaufmann (Eds.), *Innovation: A cross-disciplinary perspective* (pp. 87–137). Oslo: Norwegian University Press; Klahr, D. (2000). *Exploring science: The cognition and development of discovery processes.* Cambridge, MA: MIT Press; Klahr, D., & Simon, H. A. (1999). Studies of scientific discovery: Complementary approaches and convergent findings. *Psychological Bulletin, 125,* 524–543.

Albert Einstein quotations. Pages 76 and 92, respectively, of Einstein, A., & Infeld, L. (1938). *The evolution of physics.* New York, NY: Simon & Schuster.

Mihaly Csikszentmihalyi study of Chicago Art Institute artists. Getzels, J. W., & Csikszentmihalyi, M. (1976). *The creative vision.* Hoboken, NJ: Wiley. Michael Moore replicated the study with writers in

Moore, M. (1985). The relationship between the originality of essays and variables in the problem-discovery process: A study of creative and non-creative middle school students. *Research in the Teaching of English, 19,* 84–95.

Creativity involves problem finding. Assessments of problem finding are better predictors of real-world creativity than assessments of idea generation. See Mumford, M. D., Baughman, W. A., Threlfall, K. V., Supinski, E. P., & Constanza, D. P. (1996). Process-based measures of creative problem-solving skills: I. Problem construction. *Creativity Research Journal, 9,* 63–76. Also see Jay, E. S., & Perkins, D. N. (1997). Problem finding: The search for mechanism. In M. A. Runco (Ed.), *Creativity research handbook* (Vol. 1, pp. 257–293). Cresskill, NJ: Hampton Press; Mumford, M. D., Baughman, W. A., & Sager, C. E. (2003). Picking the right material: Cognitive processing skills and their role in creative thought. In M. A. Runco (Ed.), *Critical creative processes* (pp. 19–68). Cresskill, NJ: Hampton Press; Okuda, S. M., Runco, M. A., & Berger, D. E. (1991). Creativity and the finding and solving of real-world problems. *Journal of Psychoeducational Assessment, 9,* 45–53; Runco, M. A., & Okuda, S. M. (1988). Problem discovery, divergent thinking, and the creative process. *Journal of Youth and Adolescence, 17,* 211–220.

Pierre-Marc-Gaston de Lévis quotation. Maxim xvii from de Lévis, Pierre-Marc-Gaston. (1808). *Maximes et réflexions sur différents sujets de morale et de politique* (Vol. 1). Paris, France.

Duxon paper story. Page 39 of Byttebier, I., & Vullings, R. (2007). *Creativity today.* Amsterdam, the Netherlands: BIS. (Original work published 2002).

Steve Jobs and Apple. Isaacson, W. (2011). *Steve Jobs.* New York, NY: Simon & Schuster.

Fifteen shapes exercise. Finke, R. (1990). *Creative imagery: Discoveries and inventions in visualization.* Hillsdale, NJ: Erlbaum. The invention exercise is adapted from page 41.

Phoenix checklist. Phoenix was made famous by the former CIA consultant Michael Michalko in his 1991 book *Thinkertoys.* See pages 137–143 of Michalko, M. (2006). *Thinkertoys: A handbook of creative-thinking techniques* (2nd ed.). Berkeley, CA: Ten Speed Press.

Break It Down. This technique, often referred to as *morphological analysis,* is usually attributed to Fritz Zwicky (1898–1974), a Swiss astrophysicist based at Caltech, who wrote about the technique in Zwicky, F. (1969). *Discovery, invention, and research through the morphological approach.* Toronto, ON, Canada: Macmillan.

Draw a Fishbone. This technique is usually attributed to professor Kaoru Ishikawa of the University of Tokyo. See the history on pages 133 to 137 of Majaro, S. (1988). *The creative gap: Managing ideas for profit.* London, England: Longman.

Challenge Your Assumptions. Versions of this technique appear in many books, including Byttebier, I., & Vullings, R. (2007). *Creativity today.* Amsterdam, the Netherlands: BIS; Johansson, F. (2004). *The Medici effect: Breakthrough insights at the intersection of ideas, concepts, and cultures.* Boston, MA: Harvard Business School Press.

Reverse. This common creativity technique is found in many books, including Michalko, M. (2006). *Thinkertoys: A handbook of creative-thinking techniques* (2nd ed.). Berkeley, CA: Ten Speed Press; Nalebuff, B., & Ayres, I. (2003). *Why not? How to use everyday ingenuity to solve problems big and small.* Boston, MA: Harvard Business School Press; Wujec, T. (1995). *Five star mind: Games and puzzles to stimulate your creativity and imagination.* New York, NY: Broadway Books.

Smallpox story. Riedel, S. (2005). Edward Jenner and the history of smallpox and vaccination. *Proceedings of Baylor University Medical Center, 18,* 21–25.

Galileo space probe story. The journal to Jupiter: *The cruise—the winding road to Jupiter.* (n.d.). Retrieved from http://solarsystem.nasa.gov/galileo/mission/journey-cruise.cfm

***Whose Line Is It Anyway?* scene**. Found on YouTube at 12Medbe. (2008, March 21). Whose Line: World's worst 11 [Video file]. Retrieved from www.youtube.com/watch?v=FExVQtWjqxw&list=PLD729C21 55C9AADBE&index=11&feature=plpp_video

Hooker doll and Sheepwalk. Pages 60 and 108 of Stefanovich, A. (2011). *Look at more: A proven approach to innovation, growth, and change.* San Francisco, CA: Jossey-Bass.

Stretch and Squeeze. This common creativity technique is found in many books. The oldest source I have found is this quirky 1972 classic: Koberg, D., & Bagnall, J. (1972). *The universal traveler: A soft-systems guide to creativity, problem-solving, and the process of reaching goals.* Los Altos, CA: William Kaufmann. See page 57.

Many other creativity books contain a version of this technique, including page 57 of Higgins, J. M. (2006). *101 creative problem solving techniques* (2nd ed.). Winter Park, FL: New Management; pages 30–33 of Michalko, M. (2006). *Thinkertoys: A handbook of creative-thinking techniques* (2nd ed.). Berkeley, CA: Ten Speed Press; and Whack Pack card #22, "exaggerate."

Design scholars Singh and colleagues include this as one of their three "transformation principles." They call it "expand/collapse": Singh, V., Walther, B., Wood, K. L., & Jensen, D. (2009). Innovation through transformational design. In A. B. Markman & K. L. Wood (Eds.), *Tools for innovation* (pp. 171–194). New York, NY: Oxford University Press.

Higgins (2006) traces this technique back to Koberg, D., & Bagnall, J. (1973). *The universal traveler: A soft-systems guide to creativity, problem-solving, and the process of reaching goals.* Los Altos, CA: W. Kaufmann.

Singh and colleagues (2009) include "breaking down into components" as one of their three "transformation principles"; they call it "fuse/divide." By the way, their third principle is "expose/cover." They claim that these three (expand/collapse, fuse/divide, and expose/cover) are the only transformation principles (page 177).

Chapter Two

Ray Bradbury quotation. Strawser, J. (2011, November 29). The 90 top secrets of bestselling authors. Retrieved from www.writersdigest.com/whats-new/the-90-secrets-of-bestselling-authors

Joshua Bell story. Joshua Bell. (n.d.). Retrieved from http://info.music.indiana.edu/sb/page/normal/1593.html

Sir Francis Galton on expertise. Galton, F. (1962). *Hereditary genius: An inquiry into its laws and consequences.* Cleveland, OH: Meridian Books. (Original work published 1869).

Ten thousand hours of deliberate practice. Study of Berlin violinists: Ericsson, K. A., Krampe, R. T., & Tesch-Römer, C. (1993). The role of deliberate practice in the acquisition of expert performance. *Psychological Review, 100,* 273–305. Also see Ericsson, K. A., Charness, N., Feltovich, P. J., & Hoffman, R. R. (Eds.). (2006). *The Cambridge handbook of expertise and expert performance.* New York, NY: Cambridge University Press.

After four hours of deliberate practice, the benefits decline. Welford, A. T. (1968). *Fundamentals of skill.* London, England: Methuen; Woodworth, R. S., & Schlosberg, H. (1954). *Experimental psychology.* New York, NY: Holt, Rinehart and Winston.

Expert telegraphers. Bryan, W. L., & Harter, N. (1899). Studies on the telegraphic language: The acquisition of a hierarchy of habits. *Psychological Review, 6,* 345–375.

Chess players. Page 402 of Simon, H. A., & Chase, W. (1973). Skill in chess. *American Scientist, 61,* 364–403.

Creative people have dedicated ten years. See Gardner, H. (1993). *Creating minds.* New York, NY: Basic Books.

Vera John-Steiner interviews. Pablo Neruda quotation and Brent Wilson anecdote on page 90 of John-Steiner, V. (1985). *Notebooks of the mind: Explorations of thinking.* Albuquerque: University of New Mexico Press.

Roger Kaza quotations. Cooperman, J., How you get to Carnegie Hall. (2011, December 22). *Playbill.* Retrieved www.playbillarts.com /features/article/8639.html

People in flow are happier and more creative. Csikszentmihalyi, M. (1990). *Flow: The psychology of optimal experience.* New York, NY: Harper-Collins.

Creative learning results from concentration and reflection on what you're doing. Many studies have shown this over the years. Two of them are Auer, L. (1921). *Violin playing as I teach it.* New York, NY: Stokes; Chambliss, D. F. (1988). *Champions: The making of Olympic swimmers.* New York, NY: Morrow.

Amateurs spend their practice time in enjoyable activities that don't increase skill. Ericsson, K. A., Krampe, R. T., & Tesch-Römer, C. (1993). The role of deliberate practice in the acquisition of expert performance. *Psychological Review, 100,* 273–305.

Experts monitor and evaluate their own performance. Ericsson, K. A. (1996). The acquisition of expert performance: An introduction to some of the issues. In K. A. Ericsson (Ed.), *The road to excellence: The acquisition of expert performance in the arts and sciences, sports, and games* (pp. 1–50). Mahwah, NJ: Erlbaum; Glaser, R. (1996). Changing the agency for learning: Acquiring expert performance. In K. A. Ericsson (Ed.), *The road to excellence: The acquisition of expert performance in the arts and sciences, sports, and games* (pp. 303–311). Mahwah, NJ: Erlbaum.

Thomas Mann quotation. Page 57 of Charlton, J. (1980). *The writer's quotation book: A literary companion.* New York, NY: Barnes & Noble Books.

The flow zone for learning. Csikszentmihalyi, M. (1990). *Flow: The psychology of optimal experience.* New York, NY: HarperCollins. The "flow zone" approach to learning is often associated with Russian psychologist Lev Vygotsky and his concept of the "zone of proximal development." See Vygotsky, L. S. (1978). *Mind in society* (A. Kozulin, Trans.). Cambridge, MA: Harvard University Press.

Aalborg University. Kjersdam, F., & Enemark, S. (1994). *The Aalborg experiment: Project innovation in university education.* Aalborg, Denmark: Aalborg University Press.

The difference between experts and novices. Chi, M.T.H., Glaser, R., & Rees, E. (1982). Expertise in problem solving. In R. S. Sternberg (Ed.), *Advances in the psychology of human intelligence* (Vol. 1, pp. 1–75). Hillsdale, NJ: Erlbaum.

Steven Johnson quotation. Johnson, S. (2010, October 8). Steven Johnson: Where good ideas come from [Video file]. Retrieved from www.ted.com/talks/steven_johnson_where_good_ideas_come_from .html

Charles Darwin beetle story. Page 157 of Csikszentmihalyi, M. (1996). *Creativity: Flow and the psychology of discovery and invention*. New York, NY: HarperCollins.

Paul Maeder and entrepreneurs. Pages 50–51 of Johansson, F. (2004). *The Medici effect: Breakthrough insights at the intersection of ideas, concepts, and cultures*. Boston, MA: Harvard Business School Press.

John Mackey and reading books. John Mackey. (n.d.). Retrieved from http://topics.wsj.com/person/M/john-mackey/316

The importance of mentors. There's a correlation between having a mentor and the number of recognized creative contributions an individual makes: Nakamura, J., Shernoff, D., & Hooker, C. (2009). *Good mentoring*. San Francisco, CA: Jossey-Bass; Torrance, E. P. (1983). Role of mentors in creative achievement. *The Creative Child and Adult Quarterly*, 8, 8–15.

Most Nobel laureates have mentors. Zuckerman, H. (1983). The scientific elite: Nobel laureates' mutual influence. In R. S. Albert (Ed.), *Genius and eminence* (pp. 241–252). Oxford, England: Pergamon Press.

Famous mentor relationships. The Mentor Hall of Fame. (n.d.). Retrieved from www.mentors.ca/mentorpairs.html

Creativity techniques work better when applied to your domain. Scott, G., Leritz, L. E., & Mumford, M. D. (2004). The effectiveness of creativity training: A quantitative review. *Creativity Research Journal*, 16, 361–388.

AESOP. Suomala, J., Taatila, V., Siltala, R., & Keskinen, S. (2006, July 26–29). *Chance discovery as a first step to economic innovation*. Paper presented at the CogSci 2006, Vancouver, BC, Canada.

IDEO and T-shaped people. Brown, T. (2005, June 1). Strategy by design. Retrieved from www.fastcompany.com/52795/strategy-design. Entrepreneurs tend to be T-shaped people; see pages 50–51 of Johansson, F. (2004). *The Medici effect: Breakthrough insights at the intersection of ideas, concepts, and cultures*. Boston, MA: Harvard Business School Press.

Jeremy Gleick's daily learning hour. Page 8 of Kapp, D. (2012, January 22). Renaissance man. *The New York Times, Education Life*.

Chapter Three

Velcro story. Velcro Industries history and George de Mestral. (n.d.). Retrieved from www.velcro.com/About-Us/History.aspx; Hill, R. (1978, July). Dozens of uses for versatile Velcro fasteners. *Popular Science, 213*, 110–112.

Hasbro toothbrush story. Page 233 of Harrison, S. (2006). *Ideaspotting: How to find your next great idea*. Cincinnati, OH: How Books.

"Happy Birthday to You." Pages 233 and 235 of Harrison, S. (2006). *Ideaspotting: How to find your next great idea*. Cincinnati, OH: How Books.

Rodolfo Llinas. Llinas, R. (2002). *I of the vortex: From neurons to self*. Cambridge, MA: Bradford Books.

Henry David Thoreau quotation. This quote is from a journal entry on August 5, 1951, on page 373 of Thoreau, H. D. (1906). *The journal of Henry David Thoreau*. Boston, MA: Houghton Mifflin.

David Perkins letter blocks. Pages 79–83 of Perkins, D. N. (1981). *The mind's best work*. Cambridge, MA: Harvard University Press.

Creative people are good very good at finding exactly what they need. Page 81 of Perkins, D. N. (1981). *The mind's best work*. Cambridge, MA: Harvard University Press.

Failure indices. Seifert, C. M., Meyer, D. E., Davidson, N., Patalano, A. L., & Yaniv, I. (1995). Demystification of cognitive insight: Opportunistic assimilation and the prepared-mind perspective. In R. J. Sternberg & J. E. Davidson (Eds.), *The nature of insight* (pp. 65–124). Cambridge, MA: MIT Press.

Albert Szent-Györgyi quotation. Page 198 of John-Steiner, V. (1985). *Notebooks of the mind: Explorations of thinking*. Albuquerque: University of New Mexico Press.

Ellen Langer quotation. Page 16 and page 36 of Langer, E. J. (2005). *On becoming an artist: Reinventing yourself through mindful creativity*. New York, NY: Ballantine Books.

Richard Wiseman on luck. "Stop counting . . ." quotation is on page 29 of Wiseman, R. (2003, May/June). The luck factor. *Skeptical Inquirer: The Magazine for Science and Reason, 27*(3), 26–30. Wiseman, R. (2003); *The luck factor: Changing your luck, changing your life; The four essential principles*. New York, NY: Miramax.

Liven up the party. The lucky person's party technique is described on page 4 of Wiseman, R. (2003, May/June). The luck factor. *Skeptical Inquirer: The Magazine for Science and Reason, 27*(3), 26–30.

Look for New Patterns. Variations of this technique are found in many books, including page 16 of Michalko, M. (2006). *Thinkertoys: A handbook of creative-thinking techniques* (2nd ed.). Berkeley, CA: Ten Speed Press; pages 97–98 of Wujec, T. (1995). *Five star mind: Games and puzzles to stimulate your creativity and imagination*. New York, NY: Broadway Books. This technique was originally popularized by John Naisbitt, one of the most successful "trend spotters," in Naisbitt, J. (1982). *Megatrends: Ten new directions transforming our lives*. New York, NY: Warner Books.

"The Three Princes of Serendip." Horace Walpole told how he coined the word "serendipity" in a letter to Horace Mann dated January 28, 1754. Also see Boyle, R. (2000). The three princes of Serendip. Retrieved from http://livingheritage.org/three_princes.htm

List of accidental discoveries. Page 30 of Adair, J. (2007). *The art of creative thinking: How to be innovative and develop great ideas* (2nd ed.). London, England: Kogan Page. There's a slightly more extended version of many of these in Wujec, T. (1995). *Five star mind: Games and puzzles to stimulate your creativity and imagination*. New York, NY: Broadway Books. You can also find illustrated versions of many of them in a book for young readers: Jones, C. F. (1991). *Mistakes that worked*. New York, NY: Doubleday.

Ellen Langer's study of making mistakes while drawing. Langer, E. J. (2005). *On becoming an artist: Reinventing yourself through mindful creativity*. New York, NY: Ballantine Books. The direction to students is on page 82.

Tom Peters and strange magazines. Page 160 of Kelley, T. (2001). *The art of innovation: Lessons in creativity from IDEO, America's leading design firm*. New York, NY: Doubleday.

Japanese people seek out a bustling environment. This finding is based on surveys reported in Geschka, H. (1993). The development and assessment of creative thinking techniques: A German perspective. In S. G. Isaksen, M. C. Murdock, R. L. Firestien, & D. J. Treffinger (Eds.), *Nurturing and developing creativity: The emergence of a discipline* (pp. 215–236). Norwood, NJ: Ablex.

Henry Miller quotation. Page 25 of Miller, H. (1957). *Big Sur and the Oranges of Heironymus Bosch*. New York, NY: New Directions.

Multinationals are more creative. One 2012 study, with citations of many earlier studies with the same finding, is Godart, F. C., Maddux, W. W., Shipilov, A. V., & Galinsky, A. D. (2012, August). *A flair for fashion: Professional multicultural experience and creative performance*. Paper presented at the Academy of Management, Boston, MA.

Keep an Idea Log. I borrowed the term *idea log* from McKim, R. H. (1980). *Experiences in visual thinking*. Belmont, CA: Brooks/Cole. The story about Judy Blume is on page 75 of John-Steiner, V. (1985). *Notebooks of the mind: Explorations of thinking*. Albuquerque: University of New Mexico Press. The story about Thomas Mann is also told on page 75 in the John-Steiner book. The story about Leonardo da Vinci is on page 57 of Gelb, M. J. (1998). *How to think like Leonardo da Vinci: Seven steps to genius every day*. New York, NY: Bantam Dell.

Chapter Four

History of text messaging. I drew primarily on two sources: Wray, R. (2002, March 15). First with the message: Interview with Cor Stutterheim, executive chairman of CMG. *The Guardian*. Retrieved from www.guardian.co.uk/business/2002/mar/16/5; Introduction

to SMS and SMS messaging services. (n.d.). Retrieved from
www.activexperts.com/mmserver/sms/smsintro/

Ingmar Bergman quotation. Page 41 of John-Steiner, V. (1985). *Notebooks of the mind: Explorations of thinking.* Albuquerque: University of New Mexico Press.

John Reed story. Pages 79–82 of Sawyer, R. K. (2007). *Group genius: The creative power of collaboration.* New York, NY: Basic Books.

Exceptional creators are childlike. Pages 400–402 of Gardner, H. (1993). *Creating minds.* New York, NY: Basic Books.

Definition of worldplay and two genius examples. Root-Bernstein, M., & Root-Bernstein, R. (2006). Imaginary worldplay in childhood and maturity and its impact on adult creativity. *Creativity Research Journal, 18,* 405–425. The two worldplay examples are from page 410.

Genius quotations about adult life. Pages 416 and 417, respectively, of Root-Bernstein, M., & Root-Bernstein, R. (2006). Imaginary worldplay in childhood and maturity and its impact on adult creativity. *Creativity Research Journal, 18,* 405–425.

Gordon Gould quotation. On pages 310–311 of Brown, K. (1988). *Inventors at work.* Redmond, WA: Microsoft Press.

Vera John-Steiner quotation. Page 127 of John-Steiner, V. (1985). *Notebooks of the mind: Explorations of thinking.* Albuquerque: University of New Mexico Press.

Parallel worlds. You can find other lists of parallel worlds in several books: page 201 of Michalko, M. (2001). *Cracking creativity: The secrets of creative genius.* Berkeley, CA: Ten Speed Press; pages 232–233 of Michalko, M. (2006). *Thinkertoys: A handbook of creative-thinking techniques* (2nd ed.). Berkeley, CA: Ten Speed Press; pages 136–137 of Wujec, T. (1995). *Five star mind: Games and puzzles to stimulate your creativity and imagination.* New York, NY: Broadway Books.

Future interview technique. I found this on page 59 of Wolff, J. (2009). *Creativity Now.* Harlow, England: Pearson Education.

Carl Jung quotation ("Man's task . . ."). Page 326 of Jung, C. (1961). *Memories, dreams, reflections* (R. Winston & C. Winston, Trans.). New York, NY: Vintage Books.

André Maurois quotation. Page 64 of Maurois, A. (1950). *The quest for Proust* (G. Hopkins, Trans.). London, England: Cape.

Creative people sleep more. Pages 351–355 of Csikszentmihalyi, M. (1996). *Creativity: Flow and the psychology of discovery and invention.* New York, NY: HarperCollins.

After sleep, people are more creative. Jeffrey Ellenbogen, cited in Berlin, L. (2008, September 28). We'll fill this space, but first a nap. *The New York Times.* Retrieved from www.nytimes.com/2008/09/28/technology/28proto.html?_r=0

Seymour Cray's tunnel. Just dig while you work. (1988, March 28). *Time*. Retrieved from http://www.time.com/time/magazine/article/0,9171, 967095,00.html

Joyce Carol Oates quotation. In Oates, J. C. (1999, July 18). To invigorate literary mind, start moving literary feet. *The New York Times*. Retrieved from www.nytimes.com/1999/07/19/arts/to-invigorate-literary-mind -start-moving-literary-feet.html?pagewanted=all&src=pm

Ernest Hemingway's technique. Maisel, E. (2005). *Coaching the artist within: Advice for writers, actors, visual artists, and musicians from America's foremost creativity coach*. Novato, CA: New World Library.

Cognitive threads. Seifert, C. M., Meyer, D. E., Davidson, N., Patalano, A. L., & Yaniv, I. (1995). Demystification of cognitive insight: Opportunistic assimilation and the prepared-mind perspective. In R. J. Sternberg & J. E. Davidson (Eds.), *The nature of insight* (pp. 65–124). Cambridge, MA: MIT Press.

White, edible things. This was once one of the items on the Torrance Tests of Creative Thinking. David Perkins uses this pair of tasks on page 75 of Perkins, D. N. (1981). *The mind's best work*. Cambridge, MA: Harvard University Press.

Specificity enhances creativity. Many studies show this; here are two. First, when people were asked to think of fruits on another planet, more specific instructions resulted in greater creativity: "Do not feel bound by what fruit is like on earth" and "Be as creative as you can be." See page 207 of Ward, T. B., Patterson, M. J., Sifonis, C. M., Dodds, R. A., & Saunders, K. N. (2002). The role of graded category structure in imaginative thought. *Memory & Cognition, 30*, 199–216. Second, more specific goals were shown to result in greater creativity, according to Litchfield, R. C. (2008). Brainstorming reconsidered: A goal-based view. *Academy of Management Review, 33*, 649–668.

Tom Kelley quotation on outside-the-box thinking. Page 155 of Kelley, T. (2001). *The art of innovation: Lessons in creativity from IDEO, America's leading design firm*. New York, NY: Doubleday.

Outside-the-box training problems. Many of these are from Weisberg, R. W., & Alba, J. W. (1981). An examination of the alleged role of "fixation" in the solution of several "insight" problems. *Journal of Experimental Psychology: General, 110*(2), 169–192.

Shunryu Suzuki quotation. Page 2 of Suzuki, S. (2006). *Zen mind, beginner's mind*. Boston, MA: Shambhala Press.

Carl Jung quotation ("The creative mind . . ."). Page 123 of Jung, C. (1974). Psychological types. In H. Read, G. Adler, & W. McGuire (Eds.), *Collected works of C. G. Jung* (Vol. 6). Princeton, NJ: Princeton University Press.

Chapter Five

Stephen Spender quotation. Page 64 of Spender, S. (1970). The making of a poem. In P. E. Vernon (Ed.), *Creativity: Selected readings* (pp. 61–76). Harmondsworth, England: Penguin Books.

Aaron Copland quotation. Page 152 of John-Steiner, V. (1985). *Notebooks of the mind: Explorations of thinking.* Albuquerque: University of New Mexico Press.

Dean Keith Simonton's research. Simonton, D. K. (1988). *Scientific genius: A psychology of science.* New York, NY: Cambridge University Press.

Unusual uses. First developed by J. P. Guilford: Guilford, J. P., Merrifield, P. R., & Wilson, R. C. (1958). *Unusual uses test.* Orange, CA: Sheridan Psychological Services.

Imagine how that world is different from ours. This is called a "consequences" task, and was first developed by J. P. Guilford: Christensen, P. R., Merrifield, P. R., & Guilford, J. P. (1953). *Consequences Form A-1.* Beverly Hills, CA: Sheridan Supply; Guilford, J. P., & Hoepfner, R. (1971). *The analysis of intelligence.* New York, NY: McGraw-Hill.

Try Toppling. I originally called this technique "Zig zag," back when the book had a different working title. Once we decided to call the book *Zig Zag* I decided I had to rename this technique. I got the word "toppling" from page 40 of Byttebier, I., & Vullings, R. (2007). *Creativity today.* Amsterdam, the Netherlands: BIS. Just one of the many zigs and zags that resulted in this book!

Tony Veale referred to this as "category hopping": Veale, T. (2004). *Pathways to creativity in lexical ontologies.* Paper presented at the 2nd International Wordnet Conference, Masaryk University, Brno, Czech Republic. Also see the discussion on page 162 of Singh, V., Walther, B., Wood, K. L., & Jensen, D. (2009). Innovation through transformational design. In A. B. Markman & K. L. Wood (Eds.), *Tools for innovation* (pp. 171–194). New York, NY: Oxford University Press.

The best new ideas result from combining different concepts. Pages 114–116 of Sawyer, R. K. (2007). *Group genius: The creative power of collaboration.* New York, NY: Basic Books.

Steven Paley towelette story. Pages 85–86 of Paley, S. J. (2010). *The art of invention: The creative process of discovery and design.* Amherst, NY: Prometheus Books. The police officer quotation is on page 86.

SCAMPER. SCAMPER comes from a 1972 book by Robert Eberle: Eberle, B. (1996). *Scamper on: Games for imagination development.* Waco, TX: Prufrock Press. (Original work published 1972). Eberle based his book on Alex Osborn's verbal checklist, according to a footnote on page 108 of Higgins, J. M. (2006). *101 creative problem solving techniques* (2nd ed.). Winter Park, FL: New Management. If you like using SCAMPER, you can find an expanded list of "manipulative verbs" on page 141 of Adams, J. L. (1980). *Conceptual blockbusting: A guide to better ideas.* New York, NY: Norton. (Original work published 1974).

Unwarranted assumptions. Page 108 of Sawyer, R. K. (2012). *Explaining creativity: The science of human innovation* (2nd ed.). New York, NY: Oxford University Press.

Joe Adams kidnapping story. Cooperman, J. (2012, August). Night vision: Private investigator Joe Adams spends a cozy retirement chasing illegal immigrants through the Arizona desert. *St. Louis Magazine,* pp. 206–211, 392–397.

Daily idea time. Csikszentmihalyi, M. (1996). *Creativity: Flow and the psychology of discovery and invention.* New York, NY: HarperCollins.

Julia Cameron quotation. Page 26 of DiChristina, M. (2008, June/July). Let your creativity soar. *Scientific American Mind,* pp. 24–31.

The Artist's Way. Cameron, J. (1992). *The artist's way: A spiritual path to higher creativity.* Los Angeles, CA: Jeremy P. Tarcher.

Jeff Mauzy story. Page 154 of Mauzy, J., & Harriman, R. (2003). *Creativity, Inc.: Building an inventive organization.* Boston, MA: Harvard Business School Press.

Chapter Six

Steve Jobs quotation. Wolf, G. (1996, February). Steve Jobs: The next insanely great thing. *Wired Magazine.* Retrieved from www .wired.com/wired/archive/4.02/jobs_pr.html

Magic: The Gathering. Pages 47–58 of Lancaster, K. (1999). *Warlocks and warpdrive: Contemporary fantasy entertainments with interactive and virtual environments.* Jefferson, NC: McFarland.

Paul Howard-Jones study. Howard-Jones, P. A., Blakemore, S.-J., Samuel, E. A., Summers, I. R., & Claxton, G. (2005). Semantic divergence and creative story generation: An fMRI investigation. *Cognitive Brain Research, 25,* 240–250.

Sun Tracker beach chair. Pages 154–155 of Kelley, T. (2001). *The art of innovation: Lessons in creativity from IDEO, America's leading design firm.* New York, NY: Doubleday.

James Hampton study of imaginary objects. Hampton, J. A. (1997). Emergent attributes in combined concepts. In T. B. Ward, S. M. Smith, & J. Vaid (Eds.), *Creative thought: An investigation of conceptual structures and processes* (pp. 83–110). Washington, DC: American Psychological Association.

Mihaly Csikszentmihalyi study of ninety-six creators. Csikszentmihalyi, M. (1996). *Creativity: Flow and the psychology of discovery and invention.* New York, NY: HarperCollins.

Synectics's energy-saving roof. Pages 55–56 of Gordon, W.J.J. (1961). *Synectics: The development of creative capacity*. New York, NY: Harper & Row.

Personal analogy examples. The paper company and the reflective window examples are from Gordon, W.J.J. (1961). *Synectics: The development of creative capacity*. New York, NY: Harper & Row. The online bank example is from Kelley, T. (2001). *The art of innovation: Lessons in creativity from IDEO, America's leading design firm*. New York, NY: Doubleday. The mosquitoes and rain example is from Dickerson, A. K., Shankles, P. G., Madhavan, N. M., & Hu, D. L. (2012). Mosquitoes survive raindrop collisions by virtue of their low mass. *Proceedings of the National Academy of Sciences, 109*, 9822–9827.

The intersection. Johansson, F. (2004) *The Medici effect: Breakthrough insights at the intersection of ideas, concepts, and cultures*. Boston, MA: Harvard Business School Press.

Steelcase's Corporate Development Center. Pages 20–21 in Thompson, C. C. (1992). *What a great idea! The key steps creative people take*. New York, NY: HarperPerennial.

Seattle headquarters of the Bill & Melinda Gates Foundation. Cheek, L. W. (2012, March 18). In new office designs, room to roam, and to think. *The New York Times*, pp. BU1, BU4.

Grand Rapids Grid70. Silverman, R. E. (2012, March 21). Firms share space, ideas. *The Wall Street Journal*, p. B8.

Steven Johnson. Johnson, S. (2010, October 8). Steven Johnson: Where good ideas come from [Video file]. Retrieved from www.ted.com/talks/steven_johnson_where_good_ideas_come_from.html; Johnson, S. (2010). *Where good ideas come from: The natural history of innovation*. New York, NY: Riverhead.

Chapter Seven

Scott Adams quotation. Page 324 of Adams, S. (1999). *The Dilbert principle: A cubicle's eye view of bosses, meetings, management fads and other workplace afflictions*. New York, NY: HarperBusiness.

W. L. Gore story about guitar strings. Deutschman, A. (2004, December). The fabric of creativity. *Fast Company, 89*, 54–62; also see Sawyer, R. K. (2007). *Group genius: The creative power of collaboration*. New York, NY: Basic Books.

Purdue brainstorming study. Weisskopf-Joelson, E., & Eliseo, T. S. (1961). An experimental study of the effectiveness of brainstorming. *Journal of Applied Psychology, 45*(1), 45–49. The instructions to students are from page 46.

IDEO and brainstorming. Kelley, T. (2001). *The art of innovation: Lessons in creativity from IDEO, America's leading design firm*. New York, NY: Doubleday.

IDEO on *Nightline*. Koppel, T., & Smith, J. (1999, July 13). The deep dive: One company's secret weapon for innovation [Television broadcast]. In ABC News, Nightline.

W. L. Gore's Real, Win, Worth. Hamel, G. (2007). *The future of management*. Boston, MA: Harvard Business School Press.

Physicists and mathematicians talk about the beauty of a good theory or formula. Farmelo, G. (Ed.). (2002). *It must be beautiful: Great equations of modern science*. London, England: Granta Books.

Scientist describing simplicity ("We start off with the simple hypothesis . . ."). Page 103 of Paley, S. J. (2010). *The art of invention: The creative process of discovery and design*. Amherst, NY: Prometheus Books.

John Maeda quotation. Page 20 of Maeda, J. (2006). *The laws of simplicity*. Cambridge, MA: MIT Press.

Morse code and its alternatives. Standage, T. (1998). *The Victorian Internet: The remarkable story of the telegraph and the nineteenth century's on-line pioneers*. New York, NY: Walker.

Cranium criteria. Taylor, W. C., & LaBarre, P. G. (2006). *Mavericks at work*. New York, NY: Morrow.

Virgin criteria. Branson, S. R. (2010). *Screw it, let's do it: Lessons in life and business*. London, England: Virgin Books. Quotation is on page 191 of Linkner, J. (2011). *Disciplined dreaming: A proven system to drive breakthrough creativity*. San Francisco, CA: Jossey-Bass.

Groups are better at selecting good ideas. Larey, T. S. (1994). *Convergent and divergent thinking, group composition, and creativity in brainstorming groups*. (Unpublished doctoral dissertation). University of Texas, Arlington; Rietzschel, E. F., Nijstad, B. A., & Stroebe, W. (2006). Productivity is not enough: A comparison of interactive and nominal brainstorming groups on idea generation and selection. *Journal of Experimental Social Psychology, 42*, 244–251.

PMI. De Bono, E. (1973). *CoRT thinking*. Blanford, England: Direct Educational Services.

Gary Klein and the premortem. Klein, G. (2007, September). Performing a project premortem. *Harvard Business Review*, pp. 18–19.

Identify Three Benefits. Research for this technique comes from page 168 of Mauzy, J., & Harriman, R. (2003). *Creativity, Inc.: Building an inventive organization*. Boston, MA: Harvard Business School Press.

Devil's advocate. Woodward, K. L. (1996). *Making saints: How the Catholic church determines who becomes a saint, who doesn't, and why*. New York. NY: Touchstone.

Jon Citrin Blocker story. Page 127 of Linkner, J. (2011). *Disciplined dreaming: A proven system to drive breakthrough creativity*. San Francisco, CA: Jossey-Bass.

Chapter Eight

IDEO. Tom Kelley quotation "who make ideas tangible . . ." is from page 43 of Kelley, T., & Littman, J. (2005). *The ten faces of innovation: IDEO's strategies for defeating the devil's advocate and driving creativity throughout your organization*. New York, NY: Doubleday. Tom Kelley quotation "There's always something that wasn't clear . . ." is from page 106 of Kelley, T. (2001). *The art of innovation: Lessons in creativity from IDEO, America's leading design firm*. New York, NY: Doubleday.

Sean Corcorran story about the chair lever. Page 106 of Kelley, T. (2001). *The art of innovation: Lessons in creativity from IDEO, America's leading design firm*. New York, NY: Doubleday.

Logitech wheel story. Page 110 of Kelley, T. (2001). *The art of innovation: Lessons in creativity from IDEO, America's leading design firm*. New York, NY: Doubleday.

"Ideas evaporate unless they are massaged into reality." Page 71 of Fletcher, A. (2001). *The art of looking sideways*. London, England: Phaidon Press.

Steven Chu quotation. Chu, S. (1997). *Autobiography*. Retrieved from www.nobelprize.org/nobel_prizes/physics/laureates/1997/chu-autobio.html

Thinkering. Ondaatje, M. (1993). *The English patient*. New York, NY: Vintage Books.

Vera John-Steiner book. John-Steiner, V. (1985). *Notebooks of the mind: Explorations of thinking*. Albuquerque: University of New Mexico Press. "What nourishes sustained productivity . . ." quotation is on page 4.

Albert Einstein quotation. Page 142 of Hadamard, J. (1945). *The psychology of invention in the mathematical field*. Princeton, NJ: Princeton University Press.

Jessica Mitford and Ben Shahn quotations. Page 8 of John-Steiner, V. (1985). *Notebooks of the mind: Explorations of thinking*. Albuquerque: University of New Mexico Press.

May Sarton quotation. Pages 50–52 of Sarton, M. (1980). *Writings on writing*. Orono, ME: Puckerbrush Press.

Pablo Picasso filled up eight notebooks. In Gardner, H. (1993). *Creating minds*. New York, NY: Basic Books.

Robert Motherwell quotation. Glueck, G. (1991, July 18). Robert Motherwell, master of abstract, dies. *The New York Times*, p. A1.

Collaborative sketching. Figure 8.2 is from page 170 of Shah, J., Vargas-Hernandez, N., Summers, J., & Kulkarni, S. (2001). Collaborative sketching (C-Sketch): An idea generation technique for engineering design. *Journal of Creative Behavior, 35*, 168–198.

Movie of Pablo Picasso painting. Clouzot, H. G. (Producer, Director). (1956). *Le mystère Picasso [Motion picture]*. France: Filmsonor.

Chuck Close quotation. Page 13 of Burstein, J. (2011). *Spark: How creativity works*. New York, NY: HarperCollins.

Conclusion

Books about having ideas. Ayan, J. (1997). *Aha! 10 ways to free your creative spirit and find your great ideas*. New York, NY: Three Rivers Press; Burstein, J. (2011). *Spark: How creativity works*. New York, NY: HarperCollins; Foster, J. (2007). *How to get ideas*. San Francisco, CA: Berrett-Koehler.

Vera John-Steiner quotation. Page 79 of John-Steiner, V. (1985). *Notebooks of the mind: Explorations of thinking*. Albuquerque: University of New Mexico Press.

Acknowledgments

The book you hold isn't the one I originally planned to write, and it couldn't have been predicted when I started six years ago in 2007. The title, outline, and content have all changed many times. The only thing that's remained constant is the core concept: a book filled with research-based advice for how to be more creative. In this zig zag journey, I worked with several talented colleagues, and their contributions were essential in making the final book readable, practical, and exciting.

My literary agent, Esmond Harmsworth, has been right there with me since the path started in 2007. He closely read my draft outlines and book proposals, and offered insightful suggestions that I accepted gratefully.

Once I had a complete manuscript, Jeannette Cooperman provided me with invaluable help in polishing the text to take it to the next level. And after I completed that revision, three anonymous reviewers provided extensive and constructive suggestions that showed me how to improve the book significantly. I owe them special thanks.

The team at Jossey-Bass has been a delight to work with; they are professional, courteous, and incredibly knowledgeable about the book business. Jossey-Bass has published several wonderful books about creativity, and I'm honored to have mine join that list. My senior editor, Marjorie McAneny, was a strong believer in this project from the beginning, and she provided excellent suggestions and editorial feedback throughout the process.

Her assistant, Tracy Gallagher, was equally helpful and knowledgeable. During production, Justin Frahm and Francie Jones did a wonderful job making everything look great.

My final thanks go to my colleagues in creativity research. The best thing about my career is that I have daily opportunities for stimulating conversations and productive collaborations. This book is based on the research of literally hundreds of people, and I am grateful to them for teaching me so much.

About the Author

R. Keith Sawyer, PhD, is an associate professor of psychology, education, and business at Washington University in St. Louis. He is one of the world's leading experts on creativity, and has written or edited twelve books and over eighty scientific articles, including the award-winning *Group Genius: The Creative Power of Collaboration* (2007, Basic Books). He combines this scientific expertise with hands-on experience in real-world creativity; he has designed video games for Atari, played piano for years with Chicago improv groups, and consulted for top corporations on innovation and technology. His research has been featured on CNN, Fox News, PBS, and NPR; in *Time* magazine and the *New York Times*; and in other media. He maintains an active schedule of speaking engagements, presenting to corporations and associations, and was recently an invited participant at the World Economic Forum in Davos, Switzerland.

To join the conversation, visit www.zigzagcreate.com.

Index